Lessons Learned from Playing a Child's Game

OLYMPIC AND WOMEN'S BASKETBALL HALL OF FAME COACH

By Theresa Shank Grentz
As Told to Joan Williamson and Dick Weiss

ISBN: 1494888742
ISBN 13: 9781494888749
Library of Congress Control Number: 2014900406
CreateSpace Independent Publishing Platform
North Charleston, South Carolina

For Karl, my best friend and life partner
Karl Justin and Kevin Charles, my two finest achievements in life
—Theresa Shank Grentz.

For Fred
—Joan Williamson.

To Joan Williamson, Theresa and Karl Grentz, Mike Flynn, George Raveling, John Feinstein, Bob Ryan, Jeanine Reynolds, Pat Plunkett, Dick Vitale, and all those who stood by me when I was rebuilding my world
—Dick Weiss

Acknowledgments

Writing a book is hard work. And, like most things in life, you can't do it by yourself. Writing this book was a lot like confession. It started out, "Do I really want to do this?" It opened conversations again with people I have not spoken with in some years. Files were reopened and old stories brought back to life. Much like confession, once you go through the pains of acknowledging your many trials and tribulations, there is the joy and release of being bound by the past. There are so many people that I dare not begin to name them, but I must. My mother, Chris Shank, has been a driving force in my life and with this book. Hopefully, it will be like my trophies; my first, but not my last. Thanks, Mom, I couldn't have done this without you. I'd like to thank Dick Weiss for his support, not only with this book, but throughout my entire career. His encouragement, insight, and friendship are all irreplaceable. To Joan Williamson, who edited this book and actually knows more about my life than I do. To my friend and attorney Tracy Warren whose insight and professional advice has been invaluable throughout my coaching career. To my coaches, Maryann Nespoli, Cathy Rush, and Edith McGarry. To my coaching mentors, Billie Moore, Jody Conradt, Jill Hutchinson, Lin Dunn, the late Kay Yow, the late Sue Gunter, Howie Landa, C. Alan Rowe, and Hubie Brown. To my coaching colleagues, Chris Weller, Pat Summitt, Tara VanDerveer, Geno Auriemma, C. Vivian Stringer, Ann Meyers-Drysdale, Jim Foster, Debbie Ryan, Linda Hargrove, Harry Perretta, Muffet McGraw, Anne Donovan, Van Chancellor, Doug Bruno, the late Betty Jaynes, Beth

Bass, and Kathy McCartney. To my assistant coaches, Michael Flynn, Randi Burdick, Jean White, Bill Blindow, Nancy Gunzelman, Pat Willis, Patty Coyle, Kathleen Shanahan Shank, Kristen Foley, Telicher Austin, Mary Coyle, Gay Hemphill, Kathy Beck, Chris Dailey, Renee Reed, LaVonda Wagner, Kathy McConnell, Chris Mennig, Blaine Patterson, Stacey Terry, Marsha Frese, Ray Canaday, Krista Reinking, Pippa Pierce, and Diane Hobin. To my secretaries, Henrietta Leitner and Sandi Landeck, for all that you did for me and our programs. I could always count on you. To Ellen Ryan, the late Fr. Michael Blee, Fred Gruninger, the late Rita Kay Thomas, Ron Guenther, and Dana Brenner. To those who helped market my programs, Kevin MacConnell, Jeannie Taylor, Mike Koon, Mike Raycraft, Bill Yonan, and Mel Greenberg. Special note of thanks to Carol Callan and the USA Basketball family. To the Nike family, Phil and Penny Knight, for their dedication and support of my women's basketball programs throughout the years, the many coaching friendships fostered by the opportunity to be a part of the Nike family, Lauren Westendorf, Carole Vaughn, Eric Lautenbach, and George Raveling. To my extended family of players and their families. Thank you for sharing and allowing me and my family to be a part of your lives. There are many wonderful memories, and there is not enough space to list all of you and the many kindnesses you showed to me and my family. Thank you again. A special thank you to the following IHM's who shared their life with me and made such a difference in my life...Sister Marian William Hoben, Sister Rose Immaculate, and to those sisters who have gone on to be with their Lord, Sister Thomas Michael, Sister Kathleen Mary Burns, and Sister Mary of Lourdes. Special thanks and patience to my brothers Michael, Chuck, and Anthony who had to come after me and always answer the question: "Do you play ball like your sister?" A special thank you to my sister Donna who was always there for me, regardless of the score. Thank you for being the best siblings a person could ask for. To my Immaculata teammates who made me a star. Thanks for sharing the basketball. They were great memories and great times we shared together. We've celebrated those championships forever. And the friendships for even longer. To Buddy, Jessie, and Baxter! Paws up! To Greg Schiano, for his generosity in sharing *Finding the Winning Edge* and his passion for Rutgers. To a Loyal Son of Rutgers, Jose Carballal and his lovely wife, Rosalie, for the many hours they spent sharing their home with the Grentz' and introducing me to the fine art of how to entertain with class. Special thanks to Rob and Val Pandina for your friendship. To my sons, Karl Justin and Kevin Charles, may your lives be filled with happiness and peace. Your being there with me during the coaching years was doable because of your dedication and support of my dreams. May I be there for you in the future the way you were there for me. Thank you both. To Brian Charles, my nephew and the guy who has the next great idea. This project is possible because of your dedication and commitment to me. Thank you for making this all possible. Your passion is fabulous, and I love working with you. This is just the first of more good things to come for you! I have to remind myself every day how young you are and how you are so committed to making this our dream. Keep dreaming, B-Man, I love it!

To Kelly Wellman who will soon become the next Mrs. Grentz. Thank you for just being you.

To my father, thanks Dad for believing in me. You are my star.

Finally, to the King, Mr. Bears. My guy and life partner. Thank you for being my best friend.

* —Theresa Shank Grentz.

A special note of thanks to Steve Richardson, the executive secretary of the FWAA, my attorney Rick Troncelitti, Seth Davis, who wrote a wonderful piece on me in SI.com and John Akers, who wrote a touching editor's column in *Basketball Times*; John Cirillo, the best PR man in New York City; budding marketing star Brian Shank, Lea Miller, who is the genius behind the Battle for Atlantis, the best preseason tournament in college basketball; and good friends Dick Vitale, Howie Schwab, Sam Albano, Lesley Visser, Lenn Robbins, Roger Rubin, Larry Torres, John Paquette, Chuck Sullivan, Tim Layden, Tony Barnhardt, Chris Dufresne, Larry Dougherty, Marie Wozniak, Kenny Denlinger, Larry Pearlstein, Howard Garfinkel, Dave Pauley, Mike Aresco, Larry Wahl, Dick Jerardi, Robyn Norwood, Mike Kern, Pat McLoone, Ray Didinger, Frank Bertucci, Dana O'Neill, Malcom Moran, Ed Sherman, Jay Wright, Pat Forde, Dan Wetzel, Tom Izzo, Dennis Dodds, Tim, Andrew and

Matt Delaney, Adam Berkowitz, Elaine Ryan, Jim Lynam, Brian Morrison, Mark Blaudschun, Steve Kirchner, Dr. David Raezer, Mike Sheridan, Melanie McCullough, Craig Miller and Sean Ford from USA Basketball, Dave Goren, Kevin and Karl Justin Grentz, Dennis McNellis and Charlie, Baxter, and Jessie and the five thousand fellow journalists and folks who were kind enough to tweet messages of support back in May.

—Dick Weiss.

Foreword

"Write your book" was the simple task I wrote on the sticky note. I stuck it on her desk in the basement. The same basement decorated with plaques, pictures, medals, trophies, commemorative basketballs, and other knick-knacks acquired over a stellar four-year playing career and an unforgettable thirty-three year coaching career. "You have a story to be told" is what I would tell her. Truth be told, it was time for her to stop telling the family all her stories (as much as we do enjoy listening to them) because they needed to be shared with others. There is not a level of the game of women's basketball Theresa Shank Grentz has not touched. Whether it be winning three state championships in High School, winning the first three ever AIAW National Championships in college while being named a three-time All-American, winning championships as a collegiate coach, or winning a medal as the Team USA Olympics coach, relationships have been formed, bonds have been made, lives have been touched, and stories have been written. All because one girl dared to believe, dared to follow her passion, and dared to be great. These characteristics and ambitions have made her a legend and a pioneer to modern day women's basketball.

It takes a lot of effort to translate your thoughts from your mind on to a sheet of paper, and it takes even more effort to make the pen move. But that's why Theresa bought Dragon Dictate, a computer program that effortlessly records your speech and types it on the computer. "Speak: your Dragon is listening" was the next sticky note to appear on the desk. With a little help from Dragon Dictate, Theresa could sit in the basement on the computer and talk to herself. I know she loves to listen to herself speak! At least she had her dogs Jessie and Baxter by her side. After talking to her Dragon, Theresa could take her preliminary thoughts and present them to Dick Weiss and Joan Williamson, who worked tirelessly to perfectly compile those individual stories into one great story that has become this book.

I've known Theresa Shank Grentz my whole life; actually, she's my aunt and godmother. Fate, and a few other factors, has brought us together. Had she not hired Kathleen Shanahan in August of 1984 to be her assistant coach at Rutgers University, I might not even be here. Kathleen is my mother. In 1990, Kathleen married Chuck Shank, Theresa's brother. I was born in January 1994 in the middle of a blizzard. It was only fitting my due date was January 17, 1994, the same day an unranked Rutgers team was to play the number one ranked Tennessee Lady Vols. This story has a good ending: Rutgers won, the first time an unranked team defeated the number one ranked team, and I was born five days later. Without Aunt Theresa's hiring of my mom, and allowing her assistant coach to date her own brother, my brothers and I may not even be alive. Aunt Theresa is a mother, wife, sister, aunt, baller, coach, teacher, friend, and now, author.

Some stories make us laugh, and some stories make us cry; some stories motivate us enough to make us want to climb a mountain, while other stories help us find our inner self. *Lessons Learned from Playing a Child's Game* does exactly that, and then some. This book was carved out of values such as motivation, faith, career, passion, friendship, and family. There are many stories within stories, and many life lessons learned are shared.

Lessons Learned from Playing a Child's Game is exactly what the title implies. Theresa Shank Grentz, a decorated player and coach, is sharing the lessons she has learned during her playing and coaching career with the reader. As a teenager with budding talent, Theresa had to overcome feminism, proving she had what it took to play basketball with the neighborhood boys. And most of the time, the girl known as "Top Cat" was better than all the boys. In high school, Theresa suffered a feeling of defeat she vowed to never feel again. In college, she overcame injury in her freshman year to guide Immaculata

College to three straight AIAW National Championships, the first of any kind of championship in modern day women's basketball. She was so dominant that she was named a three-time All-American. She hung up her shoes and woolen tunic for good, and was prepared to begin her life away from basketball. But destiny would have its way, as Theresa became the head coach at St. Joseph University. Two years later, she received a phone call from Rutgers University and accepted the position to become the first full-time Women's Basketball Head Coach in the country.

In 1990, Aunt Theresa got the call she'd thought she had always wanted. She was named the 1992 Olympics Team USA Head Coach. That experience in and of itself taught her many lessons, from overcoming personal, national, and worldwide defeat to becoming a better coach and teacher on the hardwood and in life. Recovery from failing on the Olympic level took lots of support from friends and families, as well as quite a few Self-Help books. Aunt Theresa knew that if she were to continue her calling of being a coach, a fresh start was needed. She got the support she needed from the University of Illinois in 1995 and turned the program around in two short years. The Fighting Illini won the 1997 Big Ten Championship, and Aunt Theresa was named the Big Ten Coach of the Year. Aunt Theresa was on countless committees, panels, and boards, was a Founding Member of the WBCA—along with Pat Summitt, Vivian Stringer, Jill Hutchison, Colleen Matsuhara, the late Betty Jaynes, and the late Kay Yow—was inducted into the Nike Hall of Fame in 1992, inducted into the Women's Basketball Hall of Fame in 2001, and most recently was a recipient of the Joe Lapchick Character Award in 2013. Aunt Theresa put everything she had into being the best coach she could be. Because she had faith in herself and faith in a higher being, she knew when it was time for her to hang up the whistle and put down the clipboard. She retired from coaching in 2007.

From a neighborhood pickup game to the Olympic podium, Theresa has learned many lessons, and has penned (or talked to her Dragon) *Lessons Learned from Playing a Child's Game* to share these experiences with young people, athletes, coaches, parents, fans of the game, and those who need a little motivation. Her laurels stand for themselves, and it is nice when Aunt Theresa gets the recognition she deserves. She is always serving others, giving her time and talent to others, and this book does not stray from those values. This easy-read gives back; Aunt Theresa is simply sharing her experiences with those who have an interest in the game today. I hope you enjoy this book and all its stories and lessons learned just as much as I have enjoyed listening to these stories and reading this book.

That sticky note that read, "Write your book" still sits on Aunt Theresa's desk. Next time she looks at it, it might read, "Write your *next* book". Dragon, Jessie, and Baxter will be waiting in the basement to hear more of your stories.

—Brian Shank
—Theresa's Nephew

Table of Contents

CHAPTER 1

Girl Power

Always Know Your Anchors.

I believe you can be anything you want to be. You just have to have a love for something and the determination to pursue it. I was lucky. I discovered my life's passion—basketball—at an early age. I loved this game, and I wanted to be good at it, and I was willing to do whatever it took to be the best I could be.

I had a real passion for the sport.

What does it mean to have passion? How does one get passion? Is one born with it, or does one develop it? Truth be told, it is something that is inside each of us. It all depends on how much a person is willing to feed that trait in order to realize her potential.

Passion is doing something all the way. It is completing tasks. When a person has passion for something, it's all she can think about. It is all she *wants* to think about.

True passion is loving what one does and giving all the time and energy one can give to doing it. It is a complete giving of oneself to accomplishing a goal. Time does not matter; expense can be a factor, but most people will figure out a way to achieve their goals.

Ask yourself this question: "What makes me get out of bed in the morning?" When you can answer that question honestly, then you can start pursuing your dreams.

Growing up, I had a choice to make: I could stay inside and help my mother clean, or I could go outside and learn to play with the boys, and that included learning to play baseball, football, and my love—basketball.

Now, I knew how to clean, but my passion was playing basketball.

Easy choice, right?

Wrong.

When I was young, girls didn't play sports. I had to prove myself just to get into a game.

I grew up in a row home in Glenolden, a middle-class neighborhood in Delaware County, Pennsylvania. My parents were simple people who had great faith in their church, in their children, and in themselves. Family was everything to them.

My father, John, was a selector at the A&P warehouse on Baltimore Pike. My mother, Chris, was a nurse at Fitzgerald Mercy Hospital in Darby. My parents had five children. I was the oldest, followed by Michael, Donna Marie, Chuck, and Anthony.

Our house had only one bathroom. If anything, that taught us sharing and teamwork.

Our neighborhood was all boys. Joe Tomasso had two boys; Danny Menichini had two sons; and the Lentons next door had two boys.

One day, Joe Tomasso was out back, and he was having a catch with Ralph Menichini, Michael Tomasso, and David Lenton. Michael had an extra baseball glove that I used to borrow. I was standing there, and Joe Tomasso threw it to Ralph, threw it to Michael, threw it to David, then threw it back. And he missed me. I was standing in line, and it was my turn.

Boom, boom, boom.

Missed me again.

"Mr. Tomasso," "I said. "Throw it to me."

"No, Theresa," he said. "Can't. You're a girl."

Didn't throw it to me.

It wasn't just my neighborhood, either.

It was the generation I grew up in. It was a prejudice I had to overcome. I adored playing basketball, so I developed the ability to focus and stay focused.

And as I grew older, I got much better at it. So good, in fact, that I started playing with the guys. This was how I learned to be a very good player and a competitor.

I had always been competitive, but when I was in the sixth grade, I started playing against the guys. There were five boys on our block, so I was the sixth man. They were all older than me, but they let me play with them.

I was passionate about the sport of basketball. I wanted to squeeze in every last minute of playing time I could. When I was playing pick-up basketball, my father called me for dinner, called me again, and then he really called me, using my full Christian name, Theresa Marie Shank. The rest of the boys I was playing with would say, "Now you got to go." I remember constantly saying to my dad, "Two more points. Two more points, and then I'll come in." That's what passion means: I would rather play ball than eat.

I learned an important lesson: boys pick their teams based on ability; girls choose their teams on the basis of popularity. Two boys could be arguing—even engaged in fisticuffs—and although the captain might be doing battle with the best player, I guarantee he would not hesitate to pick that fellow for his team. Girls, on the other hand, choose their best friends, or the most popular, or the one who has the best clothes. It's ridiculous and not always productive.

Since I was a girl, they were very hesitant about selecting me. Once I proved myself, however, I was no longer a skirt. I was one of them. To the guy who chose me, I was the best available player. The only fellow who was upset was the one I had replaced because he wasn't good enough. He was the only guy who thought I had no business being out there playing. This particular lesson served me well during a coaching career dominated by male decision makers.

Michael Tomasso and Ralph Menichini were pretty good athletes. For me, the key was always to watch them play. Afterward, I asked them, "How did you do that?" They'd tell me, and then I'd practice the moves.

Johnny Testino was another source of knowledge. He managed to be sent to a summer basketball camp—a big deal in those days. I pestered that kid to no end. "What do they teach you at summer camp?" "What did you learn last week at camp?" "What drills or new plays have you been practicing?" After a while, he said, "TC, why don't you just shut up?" (They called me TC for Top

Cat.) This early experience not only taught me the fundamentals of the game, it also got me out of helping my mother clean the house.

A win-win situation!

We played basketball by shooting a ball through the telephone wires and the kitchen window. Ma Bell's repairmen had a fit because we separated those wires, which would cause interference on the party lines people had back then.

The service truck came by. We ran. They fixed the wires. They left.

We went back to playing.

At the time I was growing up, a girl couldn't go to a playground and play ball with the guys. And a girl was not expected to wear sneakers. God forbid that I should wear a pair of Chuck Taylor sneakers! Since I couldn't do that, I played in loafers. Just imagine how many pairs of loafers I went through! But it was worth it.

When I was thirteen, my father put up a court behind our house. There was one parking space behind each house on our block. I was always thinking, always trying to figure out a way to play basketball, and I had this great idea: "Okay, this would be so much better if this were a bigger court." I talked our next door neighbor, Mr. Lenton, into letting us put the basketball pole between the two properties.

That's where I developed my outside shot.

My father wasn't really a sports person. He took a lot of flak from people asking him, "Why are you letting your daughter play with the boys?" Even my grandmother, his mother, had reservations about my playing. She told him, "Don't let her play. It will foul up her reproductive system." It didn't faze him. He believed in me. I always knew I had my dad's love and support, so I thrived.

And my reputation preceded me.

Sort of.

Michael Arizin was a big star on the boys' team at Cardinal O'Hara High School after I graduated. He went on to play for La Salle. Recently, we were talking about old times, and he reminded me that when he was younger, he came to our neighborhood looking for a pick-up game. He asked some of my friends who was the best player on our block. "Well," they told him. "It's a kid we call Top Cat."

"I want to play him," Michael said.

"It's not a him," they told Michael. "It's a her."

It's stories like that, which never fail to amuse me.

But they are hard-won victories.

I met my husband of more than forty years, Karl Grentz, about the same time. He was our paperboy. Karl was a year older than me, and we grew up together. He lived about seven blocks away. The first time we met, I was, naturally, in my basketball uniform. He was standing on a stoop, looking up at me. He was wearing these Buddy Holly glasses and seemed, to me at least, to be rather short. Needless to say, he grew taller with the years. We started dating, if you can call it that, when I was in the eighth grade. I still remember our first date. We went to a carnival at Our Lady of Fatima Parish.

I developed a true love for the game. I feel very fortunate that I found something I loved and was good at when I was young. But I thought about how I could make myself better. I knew what I wanted and went after it, even then.

But there were all these obstacles in front of me.

I loved watching the great stars on TV. Wilt Chamberlain, Hal Greer, Chet Walker, Wali Jones, and Luke Jackson played for the Philadelphia 76ers in 1967, the year they won the NBA title. I never saw them play in person. The Spectrum was too far away. There were no female role models for me to emulate. There was no WNBA. There were no college scholarships for talented women athletes. In fact, there were very few role models for any girls back then. Even the movies we saw were stacked against independent women. Think about it; all the Disney princesses needed their princes to rescue them and give them their "happily ever after" endings.

That's why I looked for inspiration in the library.

And that's where I discovered Babe Zaharias, the great women's golfer, All-American basketball player, and former Olympic track and field star who won two golds and a silver medal in the 1932 Games. She was also an expert diver, roller skater, and bowler.

She became an inspiration for me.

She was born Babe Didrikson in Port Arthur, Texas, in 1911. At age four, she claimed to have acquired the nickname "Babe" (after Babe Ruth) after having hit five home runs in a childhood baseball game.

Already, I felt an affinity. After all, I was TC.

After she graduated from high school, she took a job as a secretary at the Employers Insurance Company of Dallas so she could play basketball as an amateur on the company's "industrial team," the Golden Cyclones. She led the team to an AAU basketball championship in 1931. But Didrikson first achieved wider attention as a track and field athlete.

Representing her company in the 1932 AAU Championships, she competed in eight out of ten events, winning five outright and tying for first in a sixth. In the process, she set four world records in the javelin throw, eighty-meter hurdles, high jump, and baseball throw in a single afternoon. Didrikson's performances were enough to win the team championship, even though she was the only member of her team.

By 1935, she began to play golf. Shortly thereafter, despite the brevity of her experience, she was denied amateur status, and so in January 1938, she competed in the Los Angeles Open, a man's PGA tournament—something a woman had never tried before. She shot 81 and 84, and she missed the cut. In the tournament, she was teamed with George Zaharias. They were married eleven months later, and lived in Tampa on the premises of a golf course that they purchased in 1951.

She became America's first female golf celebrity and the top player of the 1940s and early 1950s. If she had wanted to gain back her amateur status, she would have had to play no other sports for three years. She chose to do so, then turned pro in 1947.

And the rest is history. She won 17 seventeen straight women's amateur victories, a feat never equaled by anyone. By 1950, she had won every golf title available and 82 eighty-two amateur and professional golf tournaments in all.

Zaharias had her greatest year in 1950 when she completed in the Grand Slam of the three Women's Golf Majors of the day: the US Open, the Titleholders Championship, and the Women's Western Open, in addition to leading the money list. That year, she became the fastest LPGA golfer to reach ten wins, doing so in one year and twenty days, a record that still stands as of 2012. She was the leading money-winner again in 1951, and in 1952 took another Major with a Titleholders victory, but illness prevented her from playing a full schedule in 1952-53. Zaharias was diagnosed with colon cancer in 1953, and after undergoing cancer surgery, she made a comeback in 1954. She took the Vare Trophy for lowest scoring average, her only win of that trophy, and her tenth and final major with a US Women's Open championship, one month after the surgery and while wearing a colostomy bag.

Her colon cancer recurred in 1955, and despite her limited schedule of eight golfing events that season, she managed to gain her last two wins in competitive golf. On September 27, 1956, Zaharias died of her illness at the age of forty-five. At the time of her death, she was still a top-ranked female golfer.

In 1950, the Associated Press overwhelmingly voted for her as the "Greatest Female Athlete of the First Half of the Century," and later, she was selected the "Greatest Women Athlete" of the twentieth century.

In 1975, the film *Babe*, based on Zaharias' life, was released, with Susan Clark playing the lead role (for which Clark won an Emmy). The former NFL player Alex Karras played George Zaharias.

When the movie came out, I was all over it. I had no idea how much of it was true.

But I didn't care. What was true for me—what I cared about—was the story of a woman who had achieved athletic success. She showed me a woman could do anything if she put her mind to it and got the chance to excel.

I was determined to emulate Babe and achieve my dreams.

Early on, I did take a page out of her book. I was fascinated by how she went through the neighborhood asking the neighbors to cut the hedges at all the same height so she could practice her hurdling. In my neighborhood, everybody hung their clothes out in the backyard. You had to take your clothes down to play ball. Well, you couldn't just throw them in the laundry basket because you'd make nine thousand wrinkles in them. Some days, Mrs. Lenton's sheets blocked my double-wide court. So, we came to an understanding. She taught me how to fold fitted sheets—a skill I passed on to my sons, Karl Justin and Kevin—and I kept on playing basketball.

When I first started coaching, I didn't know that I didn't know. I remember thinking, "How would my mother do this? How would my father do this?"

I can't remember my mother and father ever fighting. They were two simple, hard-working, faith-filled individuals who believed in themselves and in each other. That bond held true for their entire marriage.

Maybe their example drew me to Karl Grentz.

When he was in high school, he always had two or three jobs going at the same time. He was a real go-getter, so it came as no surprise that he was also the only kid on the block who had money and a car.

But he had his limits when shooting a basketball. Swinging a baseball bat was another matter. Karl was excellent at that sport, but I wasn't interested in playing baseball. We played a lot of pick-up basketball on Stratford Road, and, strangely enough, his unorthodox shooting form didn't really seem to matter.

Ah, young love!

One day when I was about thirteen, I got mad playing basketball because my shot wouldn't go in. I threw the ball down in disgust and said something under my breath, or so I thought. Then, I stormed in the house and up to my bedroom. Unbeknownst to me, my mother heard me. There were thirteen stairs, and she came flying up them two at a time after me. "Who do you think you are?" she said. "You have a God-given talent, and you have no right to throw that in His face."

I will never forget that until the day I die.

I had a bad temper, I admit it.

The next day, my mother placed a poem on my dresser. It was called, "Don't Quit." It goes:

> When things go wrong, as they sometimes will,
> When the road you're trudging seems all uphill,
> When the funds are low and the debts are high,
> And you want to smile, but you have to sigh,

When care is pressing you down a bit—
Rest if you must, but don't you quit.
Life is queer with its twists and turns,
As every one of us sometimes learns,
And many a fellow turns about
When he might have won had he stuck it out.
Don't give up though the pace seems slow—
You may succeed with another blow.
Often the goal is nearer than
It seems to a faint and faltering man;
Often the struggler has given up
When he might have captured the victor's cup;
And he learned too late when the night came down,
How close he was to the golden crown.
Success is failure turned inside out—
The silver tint in the clouds of doubt,
And you never can tell how close you are,
It might be near when it seems afar;
So stick to the fight when you're hardest hit—
It's when things seem worst that you must not quit.

Many times throughout my coaching career, I gave the poem to my players, reminding them that they too have a God-given talent and things will work out; have a little patience, have a little faith. Thanks, Mom!

I had this Wilt Chamberlain Spalding basketball, and we played with it so much the bladder started to come through. One day, I became so disgusted I just left it outside. "I'm through with this," I said.

My father was watching *Gunsmoke* on TV. When he saw me, he asked where the ball was.

"I'm done with that," I said.

"Well, it might be a good time to bring it in because you might need it tomorrow," he replied. My father never screamed at me; he had a gentlemanly manner about himself when he suggested what you should do.

I went out the next day and resumed playing. Thanks, Dad!

Those types of experiences taught me a lot. My father taught me never to quit, and my mother taught me to find a way.

In addition to a love for the game, I learned to have patience and perseverance. After all, talent is something with which you're endowed. Skill is something you develop. Talent can take you only so far. There are other skills you need to get to stay on top. Teaching point: I learned to have patience through years of trial and error. When dad was sick in the hospital, my family learned patience first hand. I would sit with Dad and just be with him. My sister Donna said I would not last two minutes, but to her surprise, I could sit with him for hours. Patience can be learned. It is a skill you can develop.

When I was attending grade school at Old Lady of Fatima in Secane, we had GAC—Girls Athletic Core. Organized by the local mothers to give their daughters a chance to participate in sports, GAC was held Thursday nights in the gym at the Darby Township High School. It was a great idea because there was nothing for girls at the time. Everything was for boys. There were Little League games, parades, and CYO teams. They could be altar boys; we couldn't do that.

So, the housewives set up this program. It started with fifth and sixth graders. We registered and got a shirt. I loved wearing that shirt on Thursday nights. It was my first real sports uniform. They had gymnastics in the cafeteria. In fifth and sixth grades, volleyball was an offer. And, in the seventh and eighth grades, we played basketball. That was the plan, anyway.

Well, I wasn't waiting until seventh grade—let alone eighth—to play basketball.

I wasn't into gymnastics—too much flipping and turning. So, I ended up playing volleyball. I wasn't allowed to play basketball because the rite of passage had to be observed. But I was already playing basketball with the boys, remember? One night, at the end of volleyball, I was shooting a volleyball at the basketball rim because no one had a basketball. I was pretty good; the basketball coaches became interested in me, and I wound up on the basketball team as a sixth grader. And my basketball coach? Jean Grentz—Karl's mother.

When I first started playing, girls played with six on a side, and the rules were so different. I wasn't really that impressed with organized basketball at first. Half court, limited dribbles, two rovers. I told myself that I didn't want to play this way.

I'd cheat like mad to make it up the court in three dribbles, walking before I started and walking after I finished.

Bad Theresa!

But I must have been doing something right.

At the end of the season, we had a banquet. And I won a trophy. I thought it was two feet high. In reality, it was no higher than a glass. And that included the figurine. I brought the trophy home and set it on the bookcase in our living room where we kept our set of encyclopedias. I told my mother, "That's my first, but it won't be my last."

My mother was a graduate of Notre Dame High School, which had a tradition of great women's basketball programs—along with St. Hubert, St. Maria Goretti, Little Flower, and Hallahan. Although my mother had a health issue in her youth that didn't allow her to play sports, she certainly understood their value. And she was a competitor. She let me know what to expect on a team. She also had a favorite saying, "He who travels alone travels fastest." When we were growing up, her message to all of us was, "Don't give up. Find a way." When there was a problem, she never yelled. Instead, she would suggest, "Let's figure out what we're going to do. Let's find a way to make this happen."

When it was time to enter ninth grade at Cardinal O'Hara High School—which was a new parochial school in the area—tryouts for the basketball team were coming up, and I was, of course, nervous. Every day, my mother asked me, "Did they post the sign-up sheets yet?" And, she would always add, "If you want to be a leader, step in front. Take responsibility."

I enrolled at Cardinal O'Hara High School in Springfield, Pennsylvania, in 1965. We won three Philadelphia Catholic League championships in four years. But it wasn't always easy for me.

When I was a freshman, I became a member of the varsity team, which was very unusual. Good for me, you would think, but it caused a lot of resentment among the seniors who thought I was an upstart who just wanted to upstage them. Early in the season, we were playing a road game at St. Maria Goretti. I got in and out of the game, and the seniors were all playing, doing their thing. My concept of winning and losing was very minimal. The game was nip and tuck, back and forth, and we were losing by a point. I was on the bench when it occurred to me, Why would you lose by one point?

When I got my chance to play at the end of the fourth quarter, I took the ball and shot. I wasn't afraid of missing. And I made it.

And we won by a point.

Now, I had a choice to make. After having been iced out by the seniors, I could have chosen to be vengeful and confrontational. Instead, I opted to channel those negative feelings into positive energy. I worked hard, improved my game, and won games. I never forgot them or their treatment of me. Each subsequent championship I won, I thought, This one's for you, girls.

The seniors were so annoyed that someone had stolen their glory; they ostracized me more than they had before. When we won the Catholic League, they scribbled all over my yearbook things like, "Enjoy this championship because you won't win another one."

If they only knew.

I've always believed that a team is a family and that its members need to be sensitive to others and aware of everyone's feelings. Nothing will break team morale more quickly than knowing that the locker room needs a whipping boy, someone who will be readily sacrificed so that others can have an easy laugh.

Perhaps it's not the remarks that are said or being treated in a cold manner that's so bad. The worst is being ignored. And that's what I suffered from when I first joined the team. As a freshman, I couldn't enter the inner circle of the seniors. Coming into a locker room was a whole new experience for me. Coming into a locker room that was filled with voices and laughter that changed to a deafening silence when I got there was devastating. My classmates on the junior varsity team were having a great time, while I was struggling to master the social intricacies of girls who were three, four years older than I was—to say nothing about learning their style of play.

It was a very difficult time for me and was a situation I never wanted another player to go through.

I swore I would never have a whipping boy on my teams—if I ever had a team. The situation improved in my sophomore year after the seniors graduated. The coach during my freshman year, Edith McGarrity, resigned to get married—as single teachers did back then. She was replaced by Maryann Nespoli, a graduate of West Chester. She was our coach for the next three years, and I learned a lot from her. One of the most important lessons she taught us was owning up to one's mistakes. She told me, "Theresa, it takes a big person to admit when she's wrong." I've never forgotten those words. They are a core principal of my personal and professional life.

And they've never let me down.

• • •

Coach Nespoli was wonderfully easy to talk to. I remember sitting in her kitchen, eating mayonnaise and pickle sandwiches. Yum! She never pushed West Chester on me. Besides, I really, truly wanted to go away to school. I felt I needed to leave home for a while, to get away from Delaware County. I really wanted to see what the world held for me. She was a wonderful mentor. I remember being at the Gold Medal Tournament. Notre Dame—Ms. Nespoli's prior school—was there but had no coach present because the game was at night, and the nun who coached them had to be back in the convent by 7:00 p.m. Though employed at O'Hara, Ms. Nespoli got up from her seat, walked over to the Notre Dame bench, and coached her former players in the tournament.

To me, it was a powerful statement. It showed that she cared for those students even after she'd taken a new job. It showed her great compassion and loyalty, her ability to share her knowledge with others, and to grow as a person. It was the first lesson I learned in what a great coach could—and should—be. I took those lessons and tried to apply them to my life.

My high school career record was 49-3. I missed part of my tenth-grade season with a broken collarbone. I had fallen off the pommel horse in gym class.

When I went home and told my mother, she wanted to know what I was doing on a horse.

I returned for the Catholic League championship game when we beat St. Hubert's in March of 1968. I had a marvelous high school career; I scored over 1,200 points, made first team All-Catholic my junior and senior years, and had my No. 12 jersey retired. We won the Catholic League Championship in 1967, 1968, and 1969.

I thought it was the end of a glorious career. I wanted it to continue, but I knew I would need scholarship aid to make it happen.

I can remember reading that John F. Kennedy College in Wahoo, Nebraska, was giving out scholarships. I told my mother, "There's a scholarship available in Wahoo, Nebraska." I didn't even know where Wahoo, Nebraska was. But I was looking for that money. I wanted to make the dream happen.

In the end, I was ready to kiss my basketball dreams goodbye. I had accepted a full academic scholarship to Mount St. Mary's in Emmitsburg, Maryland to study biology.

Then, the unimaginable happened. Our house burned down on Sunday morning, March 15—the Ides of March—1970. My parents, my brother Anthony, and I were home at the time. The fire department thought it was caused by a basket of clothes lying next to the furnace that caught fire. We evacuated the house. My father had burned his hands and arms trying to extinguish the flames. Although we were all safe, the house was gone.

My parents lost everything. So did I. Maryann Nespoli had to order me a new basketball uniform before the next game because mine was lost in the fire. The uniform was there for me the next game with my number twelve—one more example of what a great coach is all about—her players!

They say that God works in mysterious ways. I'm living proof that that's true.

Before the fire occurred, my mother had made it clear that she wanted me to attend college closer to home—at Immaculata, as a matter of fact. To make her happy, I had arranged an interview on campus for that very Sunday. She'd told me earlier, "Go to Immaculata. Play basketball. Put it on the map." After the fire, I canceled the Sunday appointment. Then, a funny thing happened; it became more important to me that I stay close to my family. Later that week, I borrowed the proper suit, shoes, etc. and set out to visit the campus. The financial aid office was my first stop. But there was no scholarship money available. The good news was that I was accepted. The bad news was that I had no idea how I was going to make this work.

But I knew I would.

CHAPTER 2

That Noble Hill

*Challenges create needs and
needs create deeds.*

Immaculata was another world.

Among other things, my time at Immaculata taught me that if you are willing to sacrifice your ego for the good of your team, you can achieve goals beyond your wildest dreams.

The first Catholic women's college in the Philadelphia area, Immaculata was founded as Villa Maria College by the Sisters, Servants of the Immaculate Heart of Mary, who purchased 198 acres in Chester County and built the school on the top of the tallest hill in Frazer, Pennsylvania, thirty miles west of Philadelphia. Built in the Italian Renaissance style, the campus was secluded, serene, and quiet. It was a special place. It still is.

School history has it that Mother Camilla, our founder, looked up at that noble hill and saw a school where everybody else saw farmland. It was 1906. Women were less educated; there was no money, and they didn't have the right to vote. But Mother Camilla had a vision of a place that would educate young women to take their rightful places in the world. I think she also had an angel on her shoulder, and so she proceeded to build her school.

Mother realized that her fellow IHM sisters needed to be educated and certified if they were to instruct others. A few of them had entered the order right out of high school. She sent them out to teach and brought them back to campus to learn. She brought in professors from other institutions to teach her Sisters.

But Mother also cared about the sick and aging sisters, so she would check on the them late at night. Camilla Hall, a home for aged and infirm sisters, is named in her honor.

Mother Camilla always said she wanted to be taller.

But, in my mind, she is a giant among women.

Her motto was: "The difficult we attack immediately. The impossible takes a little longer."

These were words I learned to live by, though they didn't come easily to me at first.

In 1970, when I matriculated, the enrollment was fewer than five hundred students—I had come from a school of four thousand.

And it truly was a convent. When all the sisters came to our campus, the same rules that applied to us applied to them. We couldn't go out after 7:00 p.m. because the doors were locked. If we left by the front door, we had to be properly dressed. If we weren't, we had to leave by the back door. We had assigned places in the dining room; we didn't sit just anywhere. All of these customs were part of the IHM way. That's what they did, so that's what we did.

We had a dress code, too. It mandated that all students wear skirts and blouses or dresses on campus. This rule also stated that no skin be visible between the hem of the skirt or dress and the top of the knee socks. And, if you were seen leaving school with that skin showing, your parents were instructed to send you back to campus to change.

Oh, the rules! Those rules!

But there were also the traditions, and they were wonderful.

Charter Day, celebrated on November 12 each year, commemorates the day the school got its charter in 1920. On that day, the freshman class is invested in the college community. On Carol Night, just before Christmas, the senior class processes in academic attire, and everyone sings carols.

In short, it was a wonderful, caring place to attend college. I couldn't wait to participate.

But first I had to get there. Literally.

I still don't know how I got back and forth to campus every day during my first couple of years. It was twenty-two miles from my house to campus. That was forty-four miles a day, every day. Back then, most families had only one car, as did my family; and it was used by my parents.

I had to be resourceful. I thumbed to school at least three times a week. Then, I got creative. When I had attended O'Hara, there was a bus that would pick up students at Our Lady of Fatima, my home parish. I knew that bus stopped at Holy Cross in Springfield, and I could hop on another one that went out to Immaculata. I convinced the driver to let me off there. It was a challenge, but I did It. Getting home was much easier. Somebody had a car. Whoever drove usually dropped me off at the old Strawbridge and Clothier store at the Springfield Shopping Center, and I'd walk the rest of the way—about twenty-five minutes. If I was really lucky, I'd get a ride with Maureen Mooney, who lived in Northeast Philadelphia. She'd drive me to Glenolden before she'd go on to I-95 home.

Who does that today?

Immaculata taught me self-discipline. Now, I know that particular trait has a bad rep because of the erroneous notion that it is something unpleasant, requiring a lot of effort and sacrifice to attain. To me, self-discipline means self-control, the ability to avoid an unhealthy excess of anything that could have negative consequences. One of its main characteristics is the ability to forego immediate gratification and pleasure, in favor of a greater gain or better, long-term results—even if that requires effort and time.

And that's what happened to me and my teammates at Immaculata.

Note that word: teammates. We were loyal to one another and to Immaculata. We became a unit, and it was one of the most positive experiences of my life—one for which I'm still grateful today.

When I was in high school and college, I always believed team came first.

When the way was there but requires much sacrifice, we were there to encourage each other and even shoulder some of the load.

When it was tempting to turn back, give in or give up, we were there to say, "We can do it. We can do it."

There was never any frustration. As players, we always had the will to win. And, as a coach, my best teams felt the same way.

But the team has to come first.

That is a key piece to being on a team and building what I call virtuous friendships.

Championship teams consist of people who really care about one another; they have many virtuous friendships. When I look back through my thirty-plus years of my coaching career and the years that I played, the championship teams had that about them. Now, what does a virtuous friendship mean?

A virtuous friendship is one in which, when you are with each other, you will not disappoint. You will try to do whatever you can for each other, to be there for each other. As a result, when I look over the championship years, at Rutgers, Illinois, St. Joseph's, and Immaculata, those players and coaches—even though we don't see each other every day—once we go through the first two minutes of catching up on our spouses, family and friends, we go to where we were when those friendships began and where they remain to this day. And I think that's a special gift of a championship team—chemistry.

By the same token, when you don't have chemistry, it's no fun. There's no love. People often ask me what is my favorite memory of my career, and the answer is simple. It is when the players come back and tell me, "Now I understand why you did what you did."

That's why Immaculata was different. We were willing to sacrifice for one another. My senior year, I averaged just under twenty points a game. Scoring, to me, was not as important to me as winning another championship. In this case, our third—a trifecta.

It wasn't easy to achieve; but then, nothing worth having is.

When I was a freshman, I discovered our college didn't even have a basketball court on campus because the field house had burned down two years earlier while the school was hosting a sophomore cotillion. We had been going to the Mother House, where young women were training to become Sister Servants of the Immaculate Heart of Mary. Before we got there, the young postulants used the room for recreation. They played basketball in their habits, jumping up and down on pogo sticks, with their habits flying, or they were on roller skates. They had little pincushions attached to their habits to differentiate who was on which team during competition. After they finished, we practiced.

Do you know how slippery it is to play ball after other people have been roller-skating on the floor?

Maureen Mooney and I knew some of the young postulants, so we refereed their games before our practice.

Our coach was Cathy Rush, a West Chester graduate, and the young, attractive wife of an NBA official. We didn't even call her "Coach." We addressed her as "Mrs. Rush," even though she wasn't that much older than we were. Her initial contract with the college was for $450 annually. I don't think she ever made more than $1,200 a year. But she took the job on a part-time basis and took us, a group of players without a gym, or even regulation uniforms, to three National Championships in women's basketball.

They called us the Mighty Macs. To older, more established, more athletic teams, it probably seemed as though we came out of nowhere to win.

But, our success was based on hard work, determination, and self-discipline. There was never any frustration. As players, we always had the will to win. And that was paramount.

We had a saying. Now, we weren't into a lot of motivational things at the time; we weren't that sophisticated. We just enjoyed one another's company. And our mantra went something like this: "To play the game is great; to win the game is greater; to love the game is greatest."

But, even better, we had a prayer, which we said before every game. It was called "O God of Players," and it goes:

> O God of Players, hear our prayer,
> To play this game and play it fair.
> To conquer, win, but if to lose,

Not to revile, not to abuse.
With understanding, start again,
Give us strength, O Lord. Amen.
Please, dear Lord, if we may ask,
That all our shots go in the basket.
If we should lose by your suggestion,
The game we play, no one will question.
Matthew, Mark, Luke, and John,
Bless this court we play upon,
If we play with zeal and zest,
We will do our very best.

Later, I found out that the first two stanzas of the prayer had been composed by my Cardinal O'Hara High School coach, Maryann Nespoli, during the '50s. She was a poet and captured the feelings of a team before the game. My player at Rutgers, June Olkowski, introduced me to the last stanza.

The women of Immaculata, Rutgers, and Illinois have been popularizing it ever since.

I think it encapsulated what we believed in. We had faith in God and in one another.

And that's the truth.

We believed it, —and we proved it by becoming champions.

But it wasn't easy to get to number one.

First, there was the matter of getting dressed for the game. Our uniforms were blue woolen tunics with box pleats. We wore a blouse and bloomers underneath. They were very modest and itchy. They were cinched at the waist with a belt. We wore long white tube socks and sneakers and had corduroy jackets for warm-ups. And each of us had just one uniform. We'd play our games that way. There were no lockers, no showers, so we went home drenched in perspiration. We couldn't wash the tunics. We washed the blouses in the sink and hung them up to dry, and off we went. We didn't mind. We wore those uniforms through the 1973 season. In my senior year, we switched to skirts.

There was also the lack of equipment. We played road games at the University of Pennsylvania and at Temple University. They put their names on their basketballs to identify them. Our basketballs were a mess. Each game, we took one ball out of the opponent's bag and replaced it with one of our lousy ones. We wound up with a whole rack of everyone else's basketballs.

We had no trainer. We weren't allowed to get hurt.

When we played at Villanova my senior year, Jake Nevin, the Wildcats' legendary trainer, loved us. He taped our ankles with the pre-wrap. We watched him carefully. The next time Cathy had the First-Aid kit handy, she beckoned to us, "Come here. I'll tape your ankles." When the first player approached her, instead of using pre-wrap, Cathy sprayed stickum on the player's ankle and taped over it. The rest of us knew what to expect and politely declined. "That's okay, Mrs. Rush, I think we can manage this." We didn't have a tape-cutter and knew we'd have to pull off the tape. Ouch! One time, we played at Montclair State, and I asked their trainer how to tape an ankle.

She replied, with motions, "You put three strips here and three strips there." From then on, we taped our own ankles.

We believed in ourselves from the beginning. Then, I made a costly mistake. I forgot my sneakers on the day of the game. Dear Maureen drove me home to get them. As we were returning to campus, we were in a car accident. We finally arrived to find Cathy upset because we were late for the game. During a timeout, I whispered to my co-captain Denise Conway, "Denise, be sure to keep winning this game because I don't think I can play." I was right. I had broken my collarbone.

That was the end of my first college season. Immaculata finished 10-2.

I knew we could do better the next year, but I needed to make money to help pay for my tuition. I took a factory job, welding covers for swimming pools. That's where I decided I would never have a job where I would watch the clock. (Of course, the irony here is that, as a coach, I wound up watching two clocks: the game and shot clocks. But you know what I mean.) There were things I wanted to do in my life, and it didn't include assembly line work or buying shoes that were tied together by a string. Even after I bought the shoes, I couldn't walk in them right away until I cut the string. I wanted to buy a pair of shoes that actually came in a box and had their own individual wrappings.

There and then, I decided I was going to make enough money to buy a pair of good shoes and a quality suit. It was an investment in myself—in my future.

My sophomore year was the real break-through for our team. We had gone 12-0 by the end of the regular season. The members of that '72 team included two seniors, Sue O'Grady and Pat Opila; three juniors, Janet Ruch, Maureen Mooney, and Betty Ann Hoffman; three sophomores, Denise Conway, Janet Young, and me; and three freshmen, Rene Muth, Judy Marra, and Maureen Stuhlman.

We had a lot in common. We were all Catholics. Most of us came from working-class families. At that time, parents raised their daughters to work together toward a shared goal.

And we had one goal: to be the best team we could be and go as far as our talent and our faith in one another would take us.

The newly formed Association for Intercollegiate Athletics for Women was holding its first tournament, and it invited us to participate. We had seen the men playing in the NIT and the NCAA tournaments, and we knew all about the championships that UCLA had won under John Wooden.

But a women's post-season tournament! This was new. We had no idea we were about to become pioneers! Cathy told us, "Ladies, I want you to save your cuts for class because we're going to need them when we go to the Regionals."

We looked at one another. "Does she know where she is? You don't cut class here. The Sisters would be all over us."

(Meanwhile, the Sisters were whispering, "What's a Regional?")

The Mid-Atlantic Regional was a sixteen-team single elimination event that was held in Towson, Maryland, in 1972. We were ranked number fifteen out of sixteen teams. Today, kids fly all over the country during the summer to participate in traveling team tournaments. But, to us, this was really cool. We were honestly thrilled. We were going to stay at a Holiday Inn, and we'd never done that before.

Our second game in the Regionals was against East Stroudsburg, which was seeded second in the tournament.

Immaculata was a very close-knit college. There were seventy-six nuns on campus, and more than a few of them drove to the game. I knew they were coming, but I didn't know why they were late.

The game had already started when the gym door opened and our IHM nuns processed in, working their beads. The game action came to a halt. "What is that?" one of the Stroudsburg players asked me.

"That's our secret weapon," I told her. "And they are a large part of why you will probably lose today." I guess they had no idea that we had a higher power on our side that day. Definitely an intimidating sight to an opponent who was not familiar with the term "Sisters, Servants of the Immaculate Heart of Mary." We won, 54-48.

The sisters' prayers really helped us. Or, at least we liked to believe that was the case.

In the semi-finals, we were up against Towson State, the third-seeded team, at center court, in their home gym. What do you think the odds were?

The game came down to the wire. The score was tied, 53-53, at the end of regulation. Before the buzzer sounded, I went to shoot the ball, and I was fouled. But the officials couldn't decide if the foul occurred before the end of regulation or after the buzzer. They had the rulebook out, and they were arguing with the tournament administrators and the official timer at the scorer's table. (This was before instant replay.) Some people thought the only fair way to handle it was to play overtime.

Cathy and Ed Rush, the NBA Official, were screaming, "If it happens before the buzzer, you have to shoot the foul shots."

Twenty minutes later, I walked to the free throw line to attempt two shots. I was beginning to feel nervous, so I went to see my father who was sitting in the stands. We had a brief conversation that had nothing to do with basketball. Dad knew I was nervous and looking for his guidance. Finally, the whistle blew, and the official summoned me to the court. Dad looked at me, and ever so calmly said, "Time to go to work."

I made the first. We won the game. But I wanted to make the second foul shot so nobody could say it was a fluke.

Swish!

We were to meet West Chester the next day for the Regional title. We had played their third and fourth teams during the regular season and had crushed them both.

This time was different, and it didn't take us long to realize we weren't playing the same West Chester we had defeated earlier that season. This team was meeting us for the first time—and they practically obliterated us.

Before that game, we had decided to give Cathy flowers. The accompanying card read: "To our No. 1 coach from your No. 2 team." From that day on, we never gave flowers on game day because we thought it was bad luck. Call me superstitious, but that's the way it is.

As the winner of the Mid-Atlantic Regional Tournament, West Chester received an automatic bid to participate in the AIAW National Tournament. But, since our region was so large, Immaculata was also invited because we were the runners-up, and the only game we had lost that year was to West Chester in the Regional Championship.

So, we were off to Nationals. But first we had to finish our regular season schedule. We had one remaining away game with Rosemont College. Cathy decided to give most of the starters a rest during the game and played the rest of the team. Immaculata won 55-36. In a recent conversation, Cathy shared with me that at 6:00 a.m. the following morning, she received a telephone call from the President of Immaculata, Sister Mary of Lourdes, who was inquiring why the score was so close in the Rosemont game. Cathy told me Sister Mary of Lourdes was rather concerned with the small margin of victory and wanted to know what exactly went on in that game. (Mary of Lourdes had backed us financially to make the trip to Nationals in Normal, Illinois. She wanted to make sure we were the real deal.)

The regular season was completed, and we were off to Nationals. We had no travel budget. We had two weeks to raise money for the trip. We sold toothbrushes and raised $2,500, which was enough to send Cathy and only eight players. Cathy told three girls they couldn't go. Sue O'Grady, Betty Ann

Hoffman, and Judy Marra got the bad news, but they sacrificed themselves for the good of the team. (I still have the lovely note that Judy Marra sent the team, wishing us all the luck in the world. What a classy gesture—but typical of the type of girls we had on our team, and in our school.) Cathy had a reserved ticket. The team of eight flew standby. Recently, Cathy told me that with the team on standby, if only four or five players made the flight, she would have had to decide which players to send, again. And, if less than five players made the flight, we would have been forced to forfeit. Thankfully, we all made the flight. We got to O'Hare International Airport and drove two hours to Normal. I still don't know how Cathy rented the cars. She wasn't old enough. She was only twenty-four—and, by the way, she had just found out she was pregnant.

The 1972 Nationals were a three-day event, with one game on Friday, two games on Saturday, and the championship game on Sunday morning.

We were by far the smallest school in the bracket and the only Catholic college. The other schools brought with them assistant coaches, trainers, managers, and sports information directors. For Immaculata, it was just Cathy and the eight of us. But it was enough. (To make our team seem larger and, therefore, more threatening than it actually was, we draped our jackets on the five empty chairs on our team bench, supposedly reserved for the rest of our team.)

We won our first two games. Then, we met Mississippi State College for Women, and it seemed our Cinderella story was coming to an end sooner than we would have liked. We were down fourteen points at half. But we weren't ready to go home. Maureen Stuhlman gave the halftime pep talk, saying, "We only need seven more baskets to catch up." And we did. We triumphed, 46-43.

That meant playing West Chester. Again. The same West Chester team—Carol Larkin, Jane Fontaine, Linda Zienke, and the rest of the Golden Rams—that beat us the previous week 70-38. This time, we were to meet in the National Championship game.

But, we honestly never thought we were going to lose, and we honestly never thought we were going to win. We just knew we were going to play as hard as we possibly could.

And play we did.

The final buzzer rang out, proclaiming Immaculata the 1972 National Champions (52-48), and the news shocked West Chester, the nation, and us. We weren't sure what the winners were supposed to do, so we didn't storm the court or cut down the nets. We just stood there, looking at one another in puzzlement. At that moment, we had no idea of what had happened.

Or how our lives would change.

The one thing I do remember was that it was a beautiful spring day. We didn't need coats when we all went outside to look for pay phones so we could call our families with the news. Several years ago, I learned from Sister Marian William Hoben what it was like back on Immaculata's campus while we were eight hundred miles away. Throughout the tournament, Cathy Rush and Sister Mary of Lourdes had exchanged telephone conversations after each game. On Sunday, the college was having a symposium, and Sister Mary of Lourdes was conducting an event in a seven-hundred seat theater next to the gym. Sister Mary of Lourdes assigned one of her associates to take Cathy's call and signal to her from the back of the room thumbs up or thumbs down.

The call came. Thumbs up.

Sister Mary of Lourdes interrupted her presentation, and announced to the audience, "Ladies and gentlemen, it is my great pleasure to inform you that Immaculata College has just won the National Championship in women's basketball."

The place went wild!

Sister Marian William told me that after the announcement, cheers went up, the conference ended abruptly, and everyone on campus was scurrying to find a ride to the Philadelphia airport to meet the victors.

When we got to the airport in Chicago, Cathy's problems were just beginning. We flew out standby, so we had no tickets to come home. In the airport, Cathy and Sister Mary of Lourdes were going back and forth on the pay phone. But all was not lost; we were rescued by Cas Holloway, a successful real estate developer in Malvern and a friend of Sister Mary of Lourdes. He told her, "Send them home first class."

The West Chester team was on the same flight. At the pilot's request, they deplaned before us. We walked into a sea of about five hundred of our supporters. There wasn't a dry eye in the airport that night. Imagine being West Chester arriving home and having to walk through five hundred Immaculata fans! The truth of the matter was the players on Immaculata and West Chester were very good friends. We just had to go eight hundred miles away to play the game, while the two schools are roughly seven miles apart.

Then, we went home. A small plaque in my office reminds me daily of this amazing journey.

The day we returned to school, we posed for some public relations shots. Our uniforms smelled awful, but the PR person insisted we wear them. We didn't have our sneakers with us, so in the picture, we're wearing our long tunics and our dress shoes.

Another fashion first for Immaculata!

My only disappointment that season was the fact that we didn't receive championship rings. When I was at O'Hara, I had always wanted one. Although we were champions of the Catholic League in my freshman, sophomore, and junior years of high school, we just couldn't make it that final year—so, of course, no ring.

After we defeated West Chester for that National Championship, I thought all that might change. "We're going to get rings," I assured the team. "We won the championship. I just know they're going to give us rings!" My teammates just laughed. "Theresa, be realistic," they said. "We're not getting rings."

But I was insistent. I suppose I should have known better. At the awards banquet at the Covered Wagon Inn, Mother Claudia, Mother General of the IHMs, and Sister Mary of Lourdes presented us with rosary beads—plain brown wooden rosary beads.

The next day, I was called to Sister Mary of Lourdes's office. "Theresa," she said. "I understand you're upset."

"No," I told her. "Everything is good. I'm fine with this."

"But I was told you're a little upset," she repeated. Then, she added, "Theresa, you know those rosaries will serve you better than any ring." (Did I mention that I still have—and still use, and still love—that pair of plain brown wooden rosaries?)

Winning that first National Championship was one thing. Defending it was another. It didn't take long for people to suggest our victory was a fluke. That bothered me to no end. That's why, in my junior year, we made a point of proving we were for real. That was when we stopped being surprised with each victory and when basketball at Immaculata became more serious.

Cathy also felt she had to upgrade our talents in order for us to compete at the highest level. To that end, she recruited Marianne Crawford, a fiery point guard from Archbishop Prendergast of the Catholic League, who was considered the best high school prospect in the area. Originally, Marianne wanted to go to West Chester to major in physical education. If she had done this and teamed up with Carol Larkin (a teammate of mine at O'Hara) in the backcourt there, the history of women's basketball might have been dramatically altered. But Cathy convinced her to come to Immaculata.

Instantly, Marianne made us a much better team. Her game had a joy about it that reflected her free spirit. She was a great ball handler, a tenacious defender, and a catalyst for a lethal 1-3-1 defense that Cathy had initiated that fall. We pressed all the time that season, and Marianne made us go. We were fun to watch, since the women's game was played with a thirty-second clock, which, at times, made our games more exciting than the men's games because it eliminated stalling at the end.

Home games at Alumnae Hall were packed. To make sure there was enough seating, the girls on the team had to do some maintenance work. Prior to every game, we set up 500-600 folding chairs around the court to accommodate the ever-growing crowd of spectators.

Rene Muth's father, Lou, who owned a hardware store in Upper Darby, made sure there was plenty of noise, too. At first, we didn't have an organized pep band, so one night, he showed up with six aluminum buckets. Then, the number of buckets grew. His family carted them in on a dolly before each game, then handed them out. Before long, our parents, the Sisters, and our fans were banging on these buckets. The opposing teams and their fans needed earplugs.

We called it the "Bucket Brigade."

We beat West Chester, again, in a rematch, 63-57.

That was the day I got engaged to Karl. I remember telling my teammates about it in a huddle. He and I had become more serious in college; he was at Widener. We went to the Palestra to watch Big Five college basketball games. We talked constantly about basketball. But there was more—much more. He had a great sense of humor. I knew that if I married him, I would always be in a good mood. But I would never give him the satisfaction of laughing at his jokes. I still don't. When we became engaged, Karl didn't have money for a ring. I told him, "Look, don't buy me just any little ring. I'm telling you right now, if you don't have the money for it, that's okay. But don't buy me anything little."

In the spring of 1973, we were looking almost like professionals. We won the Mid-Atlantic Regionals and moved onto the Nationals at Queens College. There was no question that teams were gunning for us. We were no longer a cute little story. We knew that in a single-team elimination tournament, anything could happen.

And it almost did.

.We played Southern Connecticut in the finals. It was our second game of the day, and we found ourselves down twelve points, with just 3:12 to play. Thank goodness for the press. It ate away at their lead, and pretty soon, we were up by one point with forty seconds to play. Cathy called timeout and told us not to foul anybody.

So, what happened? Southern dribbled the ball up the floor, and one of our players fouled. We were lucky. The Southern player made only one of two free throws. We had the ball for the last possession, with twenty seconds left. We called timeout, but the officials forgot to turn off the thirty-second shot clock. We started a play with just ten seconds on the clock.

Marianne got confused. She was looking at the shot clock instead of the scoreboard clock. Everything was breaking down. With six seconds left, everyone was shouting for her to shoot. She put up a jumper and missed. But I grabbed the rebound and tapped in the shot at the buzzer to give us a 47-45 win.

The next day, the day of the finals, was my twenty-first birthday. "I have never lost a game on my birthday," I told the team. "And I don't intend to start now."

But we had played four games in three days.

Going into the locker room at halftime of the championship game, we were ahead. Cathy asked me, "How are you?"

I made the awful mistake of saying, "I'm tired."

She looked at me and said, "You've got all summer to be tired. Your job is to win this game."

I've never forgotten those words.

We beat Queens College, 59-52, before a crowd of four thousand to win the 1973 AIAW Tournament. They were a good team, filled with tough, street-smart New York kids. But, after the drama of the Southern game, this seemed a little anti-climatic. Earlier, we had promised Cathy an undefeated season, and we kept our pledge.

It felt good.

But I didn't.

When the game ended, everyone around me was cheering. We had lifted Maureen Mooney up on our shoulders to cut the nets. The whole time, I was thinking about next year. I moved away from the crowd, and I was sitting by myself, thinking I just played as well and as hard as I could. I averaged twenty-five points and eighteen rebounds in four games. And yet, to win a championship a third time, I knew I would have to play even better. I didn't think I could play any better than I did that week.

The celebration wasn't even ten minutes old.

From a personal standpoint, what I wanted more than anything was to go out a champion. When I took off my Immaculata uniform, I wanted it to mean something.

We were back at the Covered Wagon Inn for our year-end banquet. As we approached the dais for recognition and applause, I thought, okay, this is it. This year, they'll give us rings. No one has ever won two National Championships. This year, we're bound to get rings. Well, they congratulated us, shook our hands, but no rings and no rosaries. Their reason: "Why would we give you rosaries again? We gave them to you last year."

That fall before my senior year, I finally got a ring. Not from the school, but from Karl. Yes, it was big. And, yes, it looked terrific on my left hand.

In my senior year, our team was no longer a secret. Not only were other teams waiting for us, they were gunning for us.

They were also getting tired of us. We were the two-time defending National Champions. We were the subject of national magazine articles. Our games were broadcast on radio, and we were on local TV. That was a big deal for us.

We were being referred to as the "UCLA of the East."

It had to end sometime. And it did.

We were 54-1 and working on a thirty-five-game winning streak when we traveled to Queens College on Ash Wednesday, February 27, 1974, for a re-match of the 1973 championship game. The place was packed, with hundreds of our fans cheering us on. The final score was a tragic one, 57-56. And this unexpected loss served as gentle Lenten reminder that life's certainties are, at best, uncertain.

We rode back to campus in almost complete silence. We knew our fans would be crushed. But, when we got back, we found Sister Marie Roseanne Bonfini, dean of academic affairs, had arranged a reception/pep-rally in the rotunda. She felt it was important that the girls on the team knew that every-body cared for us, and it was okay that we had lost.

We walked in, and everyone was cheering. Denise convinced me to say a few words. "Denise," I said to my co-captain. "I thought the deal was you were supposed to take care of things off the floor, and I was supposed to take care of things on the floor."

"Well," she said. "You didn't take care of things on the floor today."

Thanks, Denise.

I took the microphone and thanked everyone for having come out to sup-port us. Then, I said, "I promise you that in three weeks, we'll bring home to you another National Championship."

Then, I put down the microphone and went home.

Denise groaned. "Why do we ever let her talk?"

But we did live up to my promise.

The National Tournament in 1974 was held at Kansas State in Manhattan, Kansas. This was the first year that the AIAW had allowed schools that gave athletic scholarships to participate in the tournament.

Our first game was against Kansas State. We played absolutely awful. I fouled out. But we survived. Then, we beat Indiana University, then William Penn College from Iowa. Finally, we defeated Mississippi University, 68-53, for the National Championship. I scored eighteen points in my final college game.

During my senior year, I scored less than twenty points a game. Why? Because I, and the rest of the team, were looking for one more—in my case, one last championship. To do that, I put my ego aside and worked toward a common goal.

Immaculata gave me a cause and taught me to be even more self-disciplined. After all I had gone through to get to school every day, I wasn't about to lose a basketball game. I became—if possible—more focused, more determined to win. When we went to those National Tournaments, the feeling of a cause grew.

My parents didn't go to our first title game because, frankly, they didn't know if we would win. In order to attend the next two, they had a fund in which they deposited their spare change, any extra money they might have. This money paid for their airfare, hotel rooms, and tickets when we played on the road. Knowing how they had scrimped and saved, I knew there was no way we I could lose. I knew we had to win, and we did.

It was time for me to hang up my sneakers, graduate, and move on.

Oh, and that championship ring? Never got it.

I had taken a full load of academic credits (fifteen) every semester. As the end of my senior year grew near, I kept getting messages from professors, telling me to get my work in. "Theresa Shank, please report to so-and-so." I really had to hustle to get it all completed because it would have been quite embarrassing if, after all the national publicity, I didn't graduate. I passed.

Our commencement was held outdoors on campus in May. It was a gorgeous day. Larry Kane, a local TV news anchor, gave the address. When I walked to the stage to get my diploma, my father, who had been very reserved at my games, got up from his seat, walked toward me, and gave me a hug. It was a moment I've never forgotten. After the ceremony, we marched to the rotunda and tossed our mortarboards in the air.

Adieu, alma mater.

I was going to be married in June. I knew my life was going to change drastically.

That year, the team that had won the AIAW championship was being rewarded with a trip to Australia in the summer to play a series of exhibition games. I had already told Cathy I couldn't make it. After the tournament, she told me that if I didn't make it, the trip was off. She told me, "They're not going to let the rest of the kids go." So, I got married, went on our honeymoon, returned home, and went to practice at camp. Karl dropped me off at the Poconos for five days. We flew out after that. Cathy was eight months pregnant with her second son, Michael, and she couldn't make the trip. She sent her assistant Pat Walsh. Billie Moore, the coach at Cal State Fullerton, stepped in for Cathy.

I had played for Billie Moore the summer before our trip to Australia in the World University Games, and I had great respect for her. When we flew back from Australia to Philadelphia, we had a day and a half layover in LA. Billie lived in Los Angeles and opened her home to us. In fact, she turned her whole house over to our team. I don't know of too many college coaches who would open their home to an opposing team, but Billie did. Just one more sign of what great coaches do—they take care of their players.

We were gone a month. It took twenty-four hours to get there. We went to New Zealand first, then Australia. We were billeted in private homes. It was a long trip, but we had a lot of fun. After we played the last game in Australia, I thought I would never touch a ball again. There were no pro leagues for women. We put our uniforms away, but I knew we would never put away our memories.

For me, it was my relationship with the Sisters at Immaculata and at Camilla that made this particular stage in my life so special. When I think back to that time, I realize there was an incredible spirit on that campus, and the Sisters were as much a part of our winning as we were.

I had a great time at Immaculata. Sister Kathleen Mary Burns once told me, "Theresa, this was your Camelot."

And it was. And still is. And always will be.

CHAPTER 3

Beginnings

"You are always useful in a job, but you are never necessary."—Mother Franciline, IHM.

I actually got my start in coaching while I was still playing at Immaculata. Our Lady of Fatima, my grade school in Secane, in suburban Philadelphia, needed a coach for their eighth grade CYO team. As a freshman in college, I found myself commuting to school, playing for Immaculata, and coaching whenever I had free time—usually on the weekends. Our first game, we lost to Holy Spirit of neighboring Sharon Hill, 50-0.

That's right. 50-0.

The second game, we played Our of Lady of Perpetual Help in nearby Morton. At least we scored this time. Final score: 52-2.

That's when I realized you could do only so much without players. So, I went down to the sixth grade and got two players—Kathleen McManus and Karen Ward. I brought them up, and I scrimmaged with the team, teaching them how to play by playing with them.

And I talked all the time.

I remember one of them asking, "Does she ever shut up?"

At the time, I didn't know how to coach. But I learned quickly.

Two years later, we went on to win the city CYO championship.

It was always an adventure. Learning how to coach was trial and error. One time, I drew up the play on my coach's little board, except I didn't tell my kids which basket to shoot at. They ran the play exactly how it was drawn up on the board. Our kid scored, but it was at the wrong basket. I looked at them and just had to laugh. I couldn't get mad at them. After all, it was my fault because I hadn't been specific about the proper basket.

I thought my coaching career would have a short life and a sweet ending after I got married to Karl in June 1974 and after I graduated from Immaculata.

Karl made the statement he was going to be the breadwinner; his wife was not going to work. Remember, this was the early 1970s—before female equality really got rolling. As a result, we lived in an apartment we couldn't afford to furnish. Rent, yes, furniture, no.

We lived with beach chairs for two years.

I was happy with the beach chairs. The first thing we bought was a brand new, hulking Zenith television set. Why? We bought this so my husband could watch the Eagles and Penn State football, with replays and analysis by Joe Paterno's older brother, George. We are Penn State. Blah, blah, blah. And he hadn't even gone to Happy Valley. He attended Widener University.

So, there we were with a huge TV set and beach chairs. But his wife was not going to work.

That didn't last very long.

There was only one bedroom in the apartment. I could clean this thing in a heartbeat. Cooking? I had done most of the cooking for our family when I was younger. Mother, father, five children, and there was always a guest or two. We had soup, salad, pasta, meat. I mean, there was a lot of food. I automatically peeled five pounds of potatoes for a meal. I made meatloaf and had a loaf of bread. Casseroles were a large part of my repertoire because you could feed more people with them.

So, when I got married, I did it the same way. Karl looked at the food and asked me, "Theresa, who is coming to dinner? There are only the two of us. You and me, count us: one, two." He said this while pointing to himself and me.

Before we got married, I did not have a taste for steak. Karl would bring steaks home from the Acme, where he worked. I had to learn how to cook steak. I had to learn how to do mashed potatoes for two. I had to learn how to do a can of string beans. So, learning to cook for two was my first problem.

Once I got married, I never ate corn flakes, puffed rice, or chicken noodle soup again.

This got boring real fast, so I decided to learn how to get creative with my culinary skills. Besides, I always wanted to go to culinary school. The Acme sold a series of cookbooks for $0.49 a week with your grocery order, and I was building a collection. One time, I thought I would start experimenting. Being Italian on my mother's side, I made chicken cacciatore for him—a spicy chicken dinner with marinara sauce. He came home, ate it, and was sick for three days.

After that, I said, that's it. I can't do this anymore. I can dust the TV, straighten the beach chairs, and make the bed only so many times a day.

We lived in Lansdowne. Karl worked in Upland, just outside Chester, and we had one car, a 1965 Dodge Coronet. He went from Lansdowne to Upton each day; so, if I wanted a job, I knew I had to find someplace to work along his route. And Fatima was on the way. So, I went to my former parish and asked if there were any teaching positions. As luck would have it, there was an opening in the sixth grade. I took the job. I got a ride to work in the morning. Karl worked at night. He drove by my classroom, beeped the horn while I was teaching sixth-grade math, and then went home to sleep. In the afternoons, I'd come home, and he'd get up and go to work.

It wasn't perfect, but it beat a day of constant cleaning and experimental cooking.

I wanted to put basketball in the rear view mirror. But it was always there, staring me in the face.

In the fall of 1974, while I was teaching, I got a life-changing call from St. Joseph's.

Father Michael Blee, the athletic director of the school, was on the phone. He had just fired Jack McKinney, who was the Big Five Coach of the Year and who had taken the men's basketball team to the NCAA tournament. As a result, there was a big stink on campus. Father Blee had been painted as a villain by the local media. But he was a hero to me when he offered me the position of part-time women's basketball coach.

I didn't say anything at first to Karl because I knew he didn't want me to get into coaching. Instead, I made an apple pie, which I knew he really liked. Then, I decided to tell him about the offer. I was making $6,300 as a sixth-grade teacher, and the salary at St. Joseph's was $1,500. The job became open because Ellen Ryan, who was coaching the basketball team, was also coaching the girls' field hockey team at Sacred Heart Academy near the St. Joe's campus.

This had been a terrible time for St. Joseph's. The Sacred Heart field hockey team was traveling in a station wagon on their way to a road game when they were involved in a fatal accident. Several of the players had been killed. The coach was not returning, which was understandable. St. Joseph's needed a coach for one year.

Because of the publicity from Immaculata's championship win, I was in demand.

I discussed the coaching possibility with Karl and went to campus for an interview. Father Blee talked to me. He was very nice and said, "Well, Theresa, your team is waiting for you in the gym." At the time, I was dressed for the interview—in an Izod dress and heels.

I thought, My team is waiting for me?

I went into the gym and, just as he'd said, there were my players, waiting for me. Here I am in my heels and a trench coat, and I could hear some of them whispering, "Oh God. There's tall. There's really tall. And there's Coach in heels."

Now, most people would say, "Well, we'll do this tomorrow" and plan for it. Me? Oh no. I'm an Aries, so I jump into the water with both feet, whether I can swim or not.

And, this time, believe me, I was treading water.

So, there I am, all dressed up, and I'm running practice. The kids are doing one drill, while I was thinking of the next drill for them to do. I was only six months older than my seniors. Mary Maley, Muffet O'Brien, Kathy Langley, and Mary Sue Garrity were all members of my first team.

I didn't know how to coach. So, I figured the best thing to do was to get on the floor and play with them. After all, a year earlier I had been playing at Immaculata, and I played against those same kids. There was a picture of me, shooting a skyhook over Mary Maley. Maryann Nespoli, my high school coach, was the referee. That would never happen today.

Mary Maley was a sophomore when I arrived. I asked her recently if my age ever came up. I was only six months older than the seniors. "No, not once," she told me. "We were so glad to have somebody who had that 'been there, done that' mystique. There was never any, 'Oh, she just got out of school,' 'Why should she tell us what to do?' That was never the case." I find that fascinating.

When I was younger, everybody always thought I was much older. I guess that was because I was the oldest of five, taking care of things, being in charge. That was my demeanor, my MO. When I got to St. Joe's, they knew I was the coach. They just did what I said. They never questioned what I said.

I was really lucky. These were smart kids, great kids. They loved life and playing basketball. They were all dean's list students. I used to joke that they held their team meetings in the library. They were going to have a good time, but I trusted them to get the job done. I wanted them to show up and be ready to play. They did. I wanted them to go to class. They did. What else was I supposed to do? They were doing what they were supposed to do. They were being college students. I wasn't one to get into their business. Even though I was so close in age with them, I couldn't allow myself to go out and hang with them. I was still their coach. And, when they came onto the court, they gave me 100 percent.

I realized it was up to me to teach them about time management. I was their coach, don't forget.

I will always be grateful to Cathy Rush for the standards she demanded from us when we were at Immaculata.

I remember that we always had to find a way to get to practice on the weekends because campus was an hour away. In today's world, kids go to practice for an hour before the game because they do rehab and get treatment. Then, they have shoot-around.

We didn't have all that. We rotated driving. Whoever had a car, made the loop, picked us up at our houses, and we made the trip to school together.

We were college students. Time management was not something we were good at. We cut it as close as possible.

Inevitably, we were late a couple of times. This really frosted Cathy because she was a stickler for promptness.

One morning, while we were commuting on the back roads of Route 252, we came across the Radnor Hunt Club doing its thing. First, we saw the fox. Then, we saw the horses carrying the Hunt members wearing their black hats and red jackets, which was all very picturesque and extremely Chester County.

Unfortunately for us, it was also very time-consuming.

We knew we weren't going anywhere any time soon. And we knew we were in big trouble—probably even more so than the fox.

When we finally got to campus, we sent Rene in to test the waters. We figured Cathy liked her. No good. Cathy was just livid. When Rene tried to pick up Eddie, Cathy's son, in his playpen, Cathy screamed at her, "Put him down."

She did.

The rest of us trooped in, and she told us to run three miles.

We did.

We tried to tell her we were caught up in a fox hunt. But she no more believed that than she believed in the man on the moon. Afterward, we were mad that she didn't believe us. And we were a couple of laps short of three miles. That night, we got together and ran the rest. We got our three miles in.

It taught us a lesson. She was the coach, and she made the rules.

Our job was to follow her. If that meant we had to leave earlier to get to practice on time, so be it. That was what we had to do. And so we did it.

• • •

Becoming a coach is not something that happens overnight. Nobody is a genius, least of all, yours truly. I was in games that we were winning, and I thought I was doing a really great job. The thing I had to learn was to stay in the moment. I had to keep thinking one or two steps ahead of our opponents.

Coaching was like a giant chess match with everyone watching and having their own personal opinion on what to do.

I was fortunate. I had great mentors, fabulous teachers. One of the biggest influences on my coaching style was Howie Landa, the coach at Mercer Community College and a member of the 1952 Lebanon Valley College team that played in the NCAA tournament. Howie won three National Junior College Championships. I used to work his summer camps in the Poconos when I was in college, and he taught me a lot about post play. He once said to me, "Therese, I teach twenty-seven post moves, but I've developed one more, just for you."

And I used it, too.

When I was selected to try out for and eventually represent the United States in the World University Games team at the end of my junior year at Immaculata, we went to camp in Iowa. The team was comprised of the best women's basketball college players across the country. We were coached by Billie Moore. My roommate for the trip was Pat Head who played for Tennessee-Martin. I called her Tennessee, and she called me Pennsylvania. Howie and Hank Slider, the legendary shooting instructor from the Lehigh Valley in Pennsylvania, were there to speak.

Howie taught offense. Hank taught shooting. "Use your first two fingers of your shooting hand, and use your pinky finger and your ring finger on your guide hand," he said. Then, to be sure we understood, he added, "The pinky finger is the one you use to put on your lipstick."

Thanks, Coach, for that beauty tip.

Seriously, though, Hank Slider taught me a lot about shooting, and I still use that knowledge today.

Howie was one of the great teachers in the game. In those days, young coaches went to clinics to listen to lectures from established men's coaches. We sat, listened, and thought it registered. When we got up and left, we realized we had missed half of what they'd said. It was hard. It was long. It was boring. But Howie was so engaging that kids loved listening to him. I loved listening to him. When I took the St. Joseph's job, I called Howie and asked, "What am I going to do with this job? How am I going to do this?"

He told me, "Therese, you're going to run a 2-3 zone, a man-to-man, and a matchup."

I told him that I didn't have a clue what a matchup was. What did I do? I drove thirty miles from Philly to Trenton to attend his practices. Picking his brain was hard, but it was worth it in the end. His point guard at the time was a kid by the name of Joe McKeown, who was a former Catholic League star from Northeast Philadelphia and is now the head women's coach at Northwestern University. One time, when Joe needed a ride home, I offered to give him a lift just so I could pick his brain about the matchup defense for two hours. I knew the point guard could explain the defense and the rules.

I went back to St. Joe's and put it in. I had brilliant kids who could run it. The matchup became one of my signatures throughout my career. People said you couldn't run the matchup all game, but we did it. We were 9-2 that first year, and Karl and I had two salaries coming in.

Another St. Joe's signature we had was a song: "Tie a Yellow Ribbon 'Round the Ole Oak Tree," by Tony Orlando & Dawn. It seemed to be on the car radio each time I left for a game. My mother made yellow ribbons for the team to wear. I felt it brought me luck.

• • •

In addition to working at the Acme, Karl made some extra money by officiating, along with his buddy Emmett Brennan, who worked for the postal service and also ran a summer basketball league.

On our first anniversary, we'd made a date to go out for dinner. I put on a little white dress, red bow, belt, and had a cute purse. On the way, Karl said to me, "I just want to stop to make sure Emmett's okay with the summer league." We stopped the car. I thought it would take ten seconds. But Karl came back and said, "Listen, Emmett is short a referee. Do you mind if I do one game? We've got plenty of time."

I figured, what the heck.

So, Karl and Emmett reffed the first game. Then, Emmett asked me a favor. The scorer hadn't shown up, and he wanted to know if I would keep score. Sure.

I'm sitting at the scorer's table. Those two are reffing the second game. Then, the third game came up. No refs showed up, so they did that one, too. We missed dinner, but I was a very well-dressed scorekeeper.

Finally, when the last game was history, it was time to go out. Emmett said, "Listen, Therese, I know you missed your anniversary dinner. I'll take you out." We wound up at a Burger King. Karl and Emmett had their officiating uniforms on. They had no money in their pockets, so you know who paid for the burgers.

Ah, married life.

Emmett was a good guy, though. When I took the Rutgers job, he lent us $10,000 for the down payment on our first house in New Brunswick. I promised to pay him back. I ran summer camp to make that happen and kept my end of the bargain. We did it in two years. Thanks, Em!

• • •

As a coach, I looked upon my job at St. Joseph's as a bridge between being a college player and becoming a coach. It acted as an incubator for my ambition. It made me ask myself, Can I do this? Do I want to do this?

The answer was a resounding, "Yes."

I started feeling I could take everything I had—my passion, my self-discipline, my experience—and put it to good use in the wider world of women's sports. I realized I could take a team of young women and help them become the best version of themselves they could be.

In hindsight, it seems like an easy decision. But, at the time, it was tricky because there weren't a lot of role models for women's basketball coaches. The game was in its infancy. Title IX had been enacted in 1972 but wasn't yet implemented.

I had my own good coaches—Maryann Nespoli and Cathy Rush—to emulate, but I needed more. I was hungry for knowledge.

And I had to get it by myself. I remember going to the library and reading books by men's coaches like Joe B. Hall of Kentucky on how to be able to play in the post. How many kids today will even Google NBA players and watch their moves? That is frustrating to me because whether you like the move or not, at least it is a sense of information. And don't forget that information is power.

I read books by John Wooden, Red Auerbach, and Bob Knight.

I was insatiable in my quest for knowledge.

I wanted to know about the history of the game. I wanted to know about the Texas Redheads, about Patsy Neal, and Carol Blazejowski of Montclair State. I wanted to know about all these people I had never seen play. I wanted to know what they did, what made them good, what made them tick.

And, I learned.

Today, when I talk to players, I don't use athletes as role models.

You know who mine are?

Benjamin Franklin, General George Patton, and Mother Teresa. That's a pretty broad spectrum but, if you think about it, what they had in common was their quest for knowledge. They had no blueprint that said how to do it, and neither did I. Their lives were inspirational to me. Benjamin Franklin's life taught me how to be an innovator. General Patton showed me how to be decisive. And Mother Teresa taught me to be truly focused and single-minded in pursuit of my goals. All good lessons learned and ones I still use.

I'm not sure if kids today know about the earlier stars in the game—people like Carol Blazejowski or Ann Meyers-Drysdale of UCLA, who won a National Championship and then got a tryout with the Indiana Pacers in 1979. But most people know about Pat Summitt of Tennessee, and for good reason.

Today, Pat is listed as the head coach emeritus of the Tennessee Lady Volunteers basketball team. She is the winningest coach in NCAA basketball history of either a men's or women's team in any division. She coached from 1974 to 2012, all with the Lady Vols, winning eight National Championships, second only to John Wooden of UCLA, who has ten. She is the only coach in NCAA history with at least one thousand victories.

In 2012, the White House announced that Summitt, who was forced to retire from active coaching after having been diagnosed with Alzheimer's, would be awarded the Presidential Medal of Freedom.

But hers was a long journey to that moment.

When Summitt was in high school, her family moved to Henrietta, Tennessee so she could play basketball in Cheatham County because Clarksville did not have a girls' team. From there, Summitt went to Tennessee-Martin on All-American honors, playing for the school's first women's basketball coach, the late Nadine Gearin. In 1970, with the passage of Title IX still two years away, there were no athletic scholarships for women. Each of Summitt's brothers had gotten an athletic scholarship, but her parents had to pay her way through college. Later, she co-captained the first women's National Team as a player at the inaugural women's tournament at the 1976 Summer Olympics, winning a silver medal. Eight years later, in 1984, she coached the US women's team to an Olympic gold medal, becoming the first US Olympian to win a basketball medal and coach a medal-winning team.

Just before the 1974-75 season, with women's college basketball still not an NCAA-sanctioned sport, twenty-two-year-old Summitt became a graduate assistant at Tennessee and was named head coach after the previous coach suddenly quit. Summitt earned $250 monthly and washed the players' uniforms—uniforms purchased the previous year with proceeds from a doughnut sale.

Summitt recalled that era of women's basketball in a February 2009 interview with *Time* magazine. "I had to drive the van when I first started coaching," Summitt said. "One time, for a road game, we actually slept in the other team's gym the night before. We had mats and our little sleeping bags. When I was a player at Tennessee-Martin, we played at Tennessee Tech for three straight games, and we didn't wash our uniforms. We had only one set. We played because we loved the game. We didn't think anything of it."

She truly was inspirational to me and mirrored the state of women's basketball in the country.

How many people today know about great women's coaches of the past like Kay Yow of North Carolina State and her fight against cancer, Billie Moore of UCLA, Jill Hutchinson of Illinois State, or Jody Conradt of Texas?

All those coaches were mentors to us.

They helped pave the way to make the game the way it is today. They made the game easier for us.

And I, for one, am very grateful.

Today, sadly, so many young players are inherently lazy.

When I was a coach, the two words I most hated to hear from a sportswriter describing my team were "lazy" and "sloppy." Every now and then, you'd get "That was just a sloppy game." That would send me over the edge. To me, there was just no room for that.

I coached at St. Joe's for two years. The first year, we went 9-2. We were supposed to play thirteen games, but two schools canceled on us. One just flat out refused to play us, and the other said we'll play you, but only if you don't play your starters. The program went from being okay to really good in a hurry. Once we added a center, Chrissy McGoldrick, the second year, we were on fire. We went 18-3. Our biggest win was over Montclair State and All-American Carole Blazejowski, a Hall of Famer. I had a brown corduroy coat and a scarf on that night. Mary Maley made a jump shot from the corner, and I raised my arms high above my head, with my fists closed. Michael Flynn, who was coaching the Philadelphia Belles, a powerful travel team that had three young stars—June Olkowski and Mary and Patty Coyle from the Philadelphia Catholic League—said to me, "Act like a dog with two bones."

After the game, the media interviewed me, and when they asked how it felt, I said, "I feel like a dog with two bones." I was simply so excited for these players because we had achieved our goal. We had dared to test greatness and made it happen. I didn't know if I wanted to stand up and cheer or just hug everyone in the building. Therefore, I felt like a dog with two bones. I didn't know what I wanted to do next.

Anyway, I was still teaching sixth grade at Fatima, and when I went in to work the next day, the forty-five kids in my class had put up a picture of me celebrating from the newspaper. It was taped all over the blackboards on the side of the classroom. There must have been forty-five copies. Every kid, including my brother Anthony, had cut it out and brought it in because their sixth grade teacher was a basketball coach. It made me feel wonderful and questioning.

I was thinking, Maybe I do want to be a coach full time because when the season was over, I was still responsible for teaching sixth grade. At Fatima, I never had detention after school because I had to coach. I thought detention was dumb, anyway. So, we never had detention in Mrs. Grentz's class.

At St. Joe's, I had a great player in Mary Sue Garrity, who led the team in scoring all four years. She had attended Archbishop Carroll High School in Radnor, Pennsylvania, twenty miles west of Philly. Mary Sue was thinking of attending Penn State University or St. Joseph's. Cathy Rush did make a recruiting call but could not offer her a scholarship. Interestingly enough, had she offered Mary Sue athletic aid, Mary Sue might have overlooked the fact that Immaculata was an all-women's school and gone there.

Mary Sue was a freshman when I took the job at St. Joe's, so I can't claim credit for recruiting her.

She was a terrific athlete. She had a job at Sears her first year in college. She made a deal with her father that she would pay half of her tuition, and her dad would pay the other half. Mary Sue worked Fridays and Saturdays and had to miss practice occasionally.

Before she entered sophomore year, I was given the opportunity to present two scholarships. My first scholarship was full tuition, and I gave it to her. It was a good thing. She later told me if another school had offered her more tuition aid, she would have transferred from St. Joseph's. I certainly didn't want to lose her over dollars. She was my best player. I split the second scholarship between two players. Everything worked out great. Mary Sue was my first scholarship athlete.

Mary Sue was never too aware of her surroundings to get nervous. She did not hear the crowd, and she concentrated solely on the next play. She never thought about losing. She just played in the moment. She played for the pure enjoyment of playing the game. She did not get rattled. She did not show signs of panic. She was one cool cookie. I can personally remember Vivian Stringer, the Cheyney State coach who went on to replace me at Rutgers and become a Hall of Fame coach, telling me that when she watched us play, she could see those cool, calm, calculating minds at work. We played Cheyney and won. You might say Mary Sue and her teammates ate an elephant one bite at a time. Not a bad way to live your life. These girls had a formula for success.

Mary Sue was a very competitive person, as was the rest of our team. However, she would compete, and even if she lost, she was very gracious, congratulating her opponents and telling them what a fine game they'd played. She was very focused and fair-minded.

When I talked to Mary Sue about her sense of fairness, she felt it came from her dad Ed, who played for St. Joseph's and was a staunch believer in the Jesuit philosophy. She spent a lot of time in the car with her father, and they had a lot of wonderful conversations. Mary Sue was the oldest of eleven children. She never felt deprived or short changed. She had a smile and a laugh that could light up an arena.

The major turning point in Mary Sue's life did not occur in college. Her family lived in St. Lawrence Parish in Upper Darby during her sixth and seventh grade years. She wasn't in the cool group; she was just another one of seventy-five kids in the class. In February of seventh grade, the family moved to St. Margaret's Parish in Narberth, out toward the Main Line. There were a total of thirty kids in the entire eighth grade. There were two classrooms, fifteen students in each. Mary Sue excelled and discovered who she was and how good she could be. St. Margaret's won the eighth grade CYO Philadelphia championship, and everyone wanted to know who their superstar was.

Mary Sue's philosophy was a simple one. *Feed me. Build me up. Give me confidence, and I will take it and run. If you are negative with me and cut me down, I will go away.* It was important for Mary Sue to be in an atmosphere that encouraged her confidence. Her father was a major influence in her success. He was an anchor for her and gave her balance, and she used his guidance to direct her life.

This is a perfect example of how a parent can be a positive influence over a child. Ed Garrity was a tough nut, but he wanted his children to be realistic about the world.

When Mary Sue was in college, her mother had a baby who was born with Down syndrome. Her family reminded me of mine. Mary Sue was never questioning. She just asked what she could do to help. Those kids were so innocent.

I didn't want them to be just great basketball players. I wanted them to be great women. I wanted them to walk in their greatness.

Mary Sue and her teammates were givers. When she played at St. Joseph's, they drew large crowds for home games. They were exciting to watch, they were successful, and people chose to come watch them play. Mary Sue was very proud of that. "Young people need confidence to excel," she once told me. "And, when they choose a school, they should select a place where they fit in and where they can play."

For me, I never thought we were going to lose. It never entered my mind.

We went to the AIAW Regionals and advanced to the semifinals, where we played against my alma mater, and I got to coach against Cathy Rush. That was a surreal experience. We lost the game to Sandy Miller and her teammates, in Pittsburgh. After that game, Kathy Langley came up to me and said, "You know, Therese, you were right. We could have beaten that team."

I wanted to flip. Don't tell me that after the fact.

I was in the Boot and Saddle when Muffet McGraw's dad, Joe O'Brien, came in. I was feeling down. To cheer me up, he bought me a martini, then another. That night, I gave up drinking martinis.

I loved the kids on that team. One of the parts of coaching I really enjoyed was watching players succeed. They came in with great hopes and dreams, only to find there were many frustrations and disappointments waiting for them on the road to achieving their great dream. But, with perseverance, single-mindedness with purpose, and the ability to take criticism, each of these young women went on to reach their dreams. I often feel like I was the mother bird, encouraging them to leave the nest and fly.

They all went on to do great things. Chrissy became a doctor. Mary Maley became an attorney. Kathy became the vice president of Scott Paper. Mary Sue founded and was president of her own insurance agency, and Muffet became the coach at Notre Dame, where she won a National Title.

Anyway, I applied for a job in admissions at St. Joseph's after the season so I could be on campus and wouldn't have to commute to my coaching job. Sister Thomas Michael, the principal at Fatima, was absolutely fabulous about the whole thing. When she asked, "Mrs. Grentz, will you be returning next fall?"

I was honest with her. She wanted to know when St. Joe's was going to make a decision. "Not until the spring," I said.

"Very well, Mrs. Grentz," she said. "We will wait for your decision."

She taught me a very important lesson about allowing people the freedom to make important decisions in their lives. From then on, whenever I hired people for my staffs, I never forced them into a hasty decision they may come to regret.

Spring came, and I didn't get the job. I told her I would be back. We really had it going at St. Joseph's. I had just recruited three really good prospects to go along with five starters. St. Joe's was selected to play in the AIAW postseason tournament. The regional games were held at Edinburgh State, in western Pennsylvania. We stayed at the hotel where Crosby, Stills, and Nash were playing. I went down to the lounge to have a nightcap and saw my team on the dance floor. Apparently, my team checked the concierge desk and saw that this new band was playing and decided to enjoy their music. They saw me and danced right out the door, never breaking stride. The next day, we won; the game was never in question. That's what I loved about that team: they knew how to love life, and they knew how to compete.

Life was good, and I was looking forward to the following year.

But, then, On August 15, 1976, my life changed. I got a call from Rutgers University. The school offered to make me the first full-time women's basketball coach in the country. They had actually offered the position to Lucille Kyvallos of Queens and Cathy Rush of Immaculata. But neither one of them wanted it. I was the third choice.

And I accepted it. This was a brave new world I was about to enter—the world of big-time women's college basketball. Rutgers, here I come.

Karl and I went to New Brunswick, New Jersey for the interview, and I signed a contract to become Rutgers' first full-time women's basketball coach. But first I had to drive back to Secane, Pennsylvania, to tell Sister Thomas Michael I was leaving after she had waited for me all that time.

I felt really bad, but this was something I had to do. I went to her office and told her I was very sorry about this, but I had accepted the job at Rutgers. I thought she was going to blow a gasket. But she didn't. Instead, she was very calm and patient and shared with me a lesson that I used for the rest of my life. I owe a great deal to this woman, and I have eagerly shared her advice with others for the last three decades.

She looked at me and said, "Theresa, always remember that you are useful in a job, but you are never necessary. We watched you. You are a teacher, but your classroom will not be the conventional classroom. Your classroom will be the world."

Now, I ask you, how profound was she?

CHAPTER 4

Accepting the Challenge

There's a fine line between being aggressive and being hostile, for women.

When I took the position at Rutgers in 1976, I never thought about what kind of resources the school was going to give me to do the job. I always expected to start out with bare bones. And that's exactly what I got. But life is full is challenges. You are defined by how you meet and overcome obstacles. I was probably too young and too naive to worry about job security. In this case, ignorance truly was bliss.

During my first interview with the media, one writer asked why I took this job and then added, "Rutgers never wins in anything, Theresa."

"I don't care what Rutgers did before," I said. "We're going to win."

I was very stubborn. The minute you told me what I couldn't do, I wouldn't argue. I'd just do what I had to do.

I may have been the first full-time women's basketball coach in the country, but I actually had two jobs. I was the head coach of the varsity and the head coach of the junior varsity. Prior to my arrival, Rutgers had no scholarships. They did not recruit. They had open tryouts for the students on campus, but no one was ever cut from the team.

I inherited a lot of athletes who played several sports. The most prominent multi-sport athlete in my mind was Kate Sweeney, who played both field hockey and lacrosse and decided to join the basketball team. She was a natural leader and served as my first co-captain. Kate was a Jersey girl and a true daughter of Rutgers. She was proud of the school and was instrumental in teaching our new players about cheers like "RU Rah Rah" and traditions like the Scarlet Knight mascot, the historic rivalry against Princeton, and the playing of the alma mater "On the Banks of the Old Raritan" after sporting events. It did not surprise me when Kate became a huge success at Morgan Stanley after graduation.

I had one part-time assistant, Randi Burdrick. Frederick Gruninger, the AD at the time, wanted me to add the assistant softball coach to my staff, but I had no interest in that. Every day, I ran the JV practice for two hours and then ran the varsity practice for another two. On game days, there were both JV and varsity games. I coached both teams in the Barn—an old gym on College Avenue in the middle of Rutgers' campus.

I was on a ten-month contract, but I got paid over twelve months, so I could keep my benefits.

One day, I went to open the gym closet and discovered someone had broken in and stolen all our basketballs.

But at least I had an office. It was in the back, but it was better than my situation at St. Joseph's—where my office was in the stairwell.

In the beginning, nobody paid any attention to us. At the time, the men's team was just one year removed from making its 1976 Final Four run. They still had great players like James Bailey, Hollis Copeland, and Eddie Jordan—who would all go on to play in the NBA. They were a hot ticket. It was exciting to watch them play. But you'd better bring anti-perspirant because it was very steamy in the tiny gym. The games were always sold out.

Finally, Randi took over the JV team so I could go out and recruit. There was only one problem: I had no scholarship. I went to our athletic director and asked for three scholarships. He told me I could have two.

That math wasn't going to work.

I was recruiting three high school All-Americans from the Philadelphia Catholic League—Mary and Patty Coyle, a pair of identical twin guards from West Catholic, and June Olkowski, a six-foot forward from St. Maria Goretti.

I thought they could take Rutgers to the next level—from playing teams like Keane, Trenton State, and Glassboro in the New Jersey Conference, to competing for a National Championship.

That was my goal.

I had been really good friends with these kids before I recruited them and really thought we could get them.

I sweated it out all winter. Every day, I would go by Fred's office and ask his administrative assistant what kind of a mood he was in. Even though I didn't have the scholarships, I kept recruiting them. The twins had made visits to many schools. They had been to Old Dominion, a national power, which was coached by my former college teammate, Marianne Crawford, and had two All-Americans, Nancy Lieberman and six foot, five inch Inge Nissen.

Frankly, I was worried.

Finally, Patty pulled the trigger. She told Mary, "I don't care what you do. I'm going to Rutgers."

Mary said, "Okay."

Two down. One to go.

By spring, I had convinced Rutgers to give me that third ride. I got a little concerned when June made her official visit at the end of the winter. "It's so brown. There's no green," June told her parents.

"What did you expect?" her sister, Gail, said. "It's March."

When the sun finally came out and June committed, we sent her a National Letter of Intent. And we spelled her name wrong. Her late father, Chuck, never let me forget about that. Bad!

The twins had played for West Catholic and Dolores Purcell, along with their older sister, Kathy. Their teammate was Rene Dunne, who went on to become a star at St. Joseph's. Like me, they were products of the playgrounds, in their case competing against boys in Southwest Philadelphia.

One time, when they were in eighth grade and playing for Good Shepherd CYO, the boys on the eighth grade team were razzing them, saying girls couldn't play. So, Mary and Patty grabbed their sister, Kathy, and challenged the boys to a game of three-on-three. They beat them just to prove a point.

The three sisters won the Catholic League title when the twins were juniors and Kathy was a senior. They lived in a row house with their parents, John and Bunny, and six siblings. They used to practice their ball handling in the basement. The house had only one bathroom—just like in my house. There were five girls—Kathy, Mary, Patty, Elaine, and Maureen—and three boys—Johnny, Jimmy, and Kevin. If nothing else, having that large a family taught them teamwork. There were two sets of bunk beds in one room. So, when the twins went to college and lived with only one other person, it was an upgrade. Today, students have their own room and their own bathroom at home. When they go to college and live with someone else, it's a downgrade.

They were like my little sisters. They used to ride their bikes five miles to my apartment in Lansdowne. I always had candy for them. No furniture, but plenty of candy and a big TV. They were fortunate. They always had people in their lives looking after them.

June was a trip. She was from South Philly. She was the youngest of four children and grew up in a row house around the corner from a playground. "No backyard," she said. "And cement in the front." She remembers her mother, Eleanor, tying her pigtails in bows and sending her out to shoot hoops. She was a natural.

When June was in ninth grade at St. Maria Goretti, she sent me a picture and asked if I would autograph it. I remember writing to her, "June, if you are going to wear pigtails, you'd better be good." Most South Philly kids were street smart. June wasn't. She was the baby of the family and loved her parents. When her dad died, she gave a beautiful and touching eulogy but true to form for June, with a touch of humor. I still remember her saying, "The reason I'm up here instead of one of my siblings is that they once told me this was the only way I could get to the altar at Mt. Carmel church with my father."

June had an effervescence about her. When she came into a room, she lit it up. And she could play. In high school, she made the USA team as a junior, won the Catholic League as a senior, and was a Parade All-American, along with the twins, that same year. I was close with the Philly kids. I wasn't really a mother or father figure to them, I was more of an older sister. They would call, asking if I had gone food shopping. Then, they would come over and raid the pantry. June would come on Tuesday mornings and make French toast, and it was very good. June taught me how to make her version of French toast, and my oldest son, Karl, loved it. I continued to make it for all my nephews. One day, my nephew, Brian, told his mother, Kathleen, that she doesn't make French toast the way Aunt Theresa does. Thanks, June!

That is not to say there weren't growing pains.

Mary was the calm one with a perfect point guard's mentality. Patty could really shoot it, but she had an intensity about her. June was bubbly.

When Patty was a freshman, I threw her out of practice before the season started because she dropped a four-letter word. She got so mad she stormed back to her dorm room and told Mary, "Pack your bags. We're leaving." But they were ten dollars short of a train ticket. Patty walked down to the end of the hall in the dorm and called her mother.

But Bunny would have none of it.

"No," she told Patty. "You've made your decision, and you're going to stick with it."

Then, she hung up on her.

When Patty went back to her room, Mary asked her what happened. Then added, "I'm packed."

Patty told Mary that their mother had just hung up on her. They wound up unpacking. (It's nice when parents have your back.) The next day, Patty was back at practice when another player dropped a curse word. She was all over me. "What are you going to do about that, Therese?" she asked.

"Patty," I said. "Would you say that on Dolores Purcell's court at West Catholic?" referring to her high school coach.

"No," Patty said.

"Well, you're not going to do that on mine, either," I told her.

And that was the end of that.

I knew that when June and the twins enrolled in 1978, I had the nucleus of a team that could eventually make a run at a National Championship. But first, I had to take care of some personal business. That fall, I was pregnant with our first son, Karl Justin, but I coached very close to my delivery date in November.

I was huge. I was two weeks late, and I never dropped because I had all these muscles in my stomach, or so they told me. I hadn't delivered yet, and we had a scrimmage against Army. Karl and Emmett took the team to West Point and coached the scrimmage on a Saturday. I remained home because I couldn't travel. Wish I could have been there to see our team eating in the cafeteria with 1,800 cadets.

Monday, I started to get funny looking, according Emmett, who was staying with us.

He fled. Karl was working the night shift. The contractions started earlier in the evening, but I was in no rush and waited a few more hours. After midnight, I called Karl and asked him to take me to the hospital. But he couldn't get home in time because of a heavy fog that had settled over the area.

I walked two blocks to the hospital emergency room, sat myself down in a wheelchair, and waited for Karl.

Karl Justin was a big baby, weighing in at ten pounds, nine ounces. I always knew when the nurses were bringing him to my room because I could hear him crying. They didn't give him just one bottle. They gave him two.

Late one night, my players decided to visit my towheaded son and me, so they sneaked up the back stairway of the hospital. They had a six-pack. They were having a blast. I sent them home because I needed sleep.

Fast forward: In 2012, I was giving a leadership speech to women attorneys in North Jersey. There was one gentleman in the group. He came up and said, "'You don't remember me; but you and my mother were roommates when you both gave birth." His name is Kevin I. Asadi. His parents are Leila and Mac Asadi. And he was born on November 7, 1978, the same day as Karl Justin Grentz was born. He refers to himself as my "maternity ward nephew."

Small world.

After I came back to work, we went to play St. John's in an early season road game. They had these big steps in their arena that led to the visiting locker room. I looked at those steps and told my team, "No way. I'm not doing those steps." We went behind the bleachers, and I said, "That's as far as we're going. We're having our halftime talk right here."

And we did.

Our first home game that year was against Northwestern. I still remember putting June in for the first time. She promptly got her shot blocked.

When she came out, I said to her, "Welcome to Division I."

We won that game and twenty-seven more, finishing 28-4. We were ranked seventh in the country. June and the twins eventually figured out how to play because they were used to working things out by themselves. They were entering a new phase of their lives. They were meeting new people. Nobody ran interference for them. They just understood the game. Those three would pass up good shots to get great ones. People don't do that today. People rush and take bad shots. They could run my offense and go through six or seven options until they got the shot they wanted.

They were the missing pieces of a team that had won eighteen games the previous year and had some good young players from Lehigh Valley in Patti Sikorski and Kathy Glutz, who were from Allentown and Pottstown, Pennsylvania, and originally had been all set to play for me at St. Joseph's, but changed their minds when I went to Rutgers. I also had Sandy Tupurins, a six foot, four inch center from Metuchen, New Jersey, who came because she read the article about Immaculata beating Queens in our second National Championship game in *Sports Illustrated*. She still holds the school record with twenty-six rebounds in a game. I played with my teams at Rutgers and wasn't bad. One day, I was chasing Sandy down the floor and couldn't catch her, so I reached for her and grabbed her shorts. Two plays later, I was yelling at her for not rebounding and getting her hands up. She looked at me and said, "Coach, I would love to rebound for you, but I have to hold up my pants, you ripped the elastic out of my underwear on that grab you made two plays ago."

Bad Theresa!

I did replace her special panties with new lingerie, along with the word "string beans" on the leg—string beans were "Tupes" secret weapon she ate before games.

I wanted to upgrade our schedule. But, again, I got resistance from the AD, who balked at the idea. "This is good enough for you," he told me. He didn't want this team to get too big. After all, we were just a women's team.

But my vision certainly didn't mirror his. I thought the bigger, the better. The sky's the limit.

I just kept pushing. I tried to do it gently. I tried to do it diplomatically. But I had to keep pushing because I decided that if Karl and I were committed to living in New Jersey, away from our parents and friends, I wasn't going to do this half-heartedly. After the twins and June arrived, we just killed the Jersey state schools. The scores were atrociously lop-sided. I figured if the scores got bad enough, the AD would realize his attitude wasn't helping anyone.

But that never happened.

We built the program to a point where we finished in the top ten for four straight years. The first ever women's Top 25 was compiled by Mel Greenberg, who worked in the sports department at the *Philadelphia Inquirer*, in 1976. It was a true labor of love and helped pioneer national coverage of the sport. Nobody knew what was going in other regions at the time because AP didn't even carry our scores on the wire. But Mel was willing to do the research. He would call coaches from around the country and either he or the interns he recruited would read off the scores from the top teams, and then Mel would call back an hour later and take our votes. My call usually came shortly after *Wonderful World of Disney* on Sunday nights. It was a three-hour process. You had to keep tabs on the way you voted every week during the season. I still don't know how he got it done in time for Tuesday release. As time went on and Karl Justin got a little older, I trained him to take down all the scores. Karl got really good at it, which cut down my time on the phone. I also got a fax machine to send in my ballot so I could get to bed before midnight.

Eventually, in 1986, the WBCA sponsored a women's Top 25 poll, and the AP started a poll of its own. But the women's coaches were so appreciative of what Mel did for the sport in its infancy that he was inducted into the Women's Basketball Hall of Fame in 2007.

We were dangerous back in those days. Teams were afraid to play us zone because we had so many shooters—Patty Delehanty, Patty Coyle, Denise Kenney, and Joanne Burke. Fans became interested in us because we played doubleheaders with the men at the Rutgers Athletic Center, which opened in 1977. We played at 6:00 p.m. The men played at 8:00 p.m. After a while, we noticed that people started coming in earlier to catch the tail end of our games. One time, we ran a play off a double stack for a shooter. I can remember Tom Young, the men's coach, saying to his assistant, Joe Boylan, "How the hell do they always make that shot?"

It was hard not to like our kids. They were such hams. They always talked to people, and our booster club loved them. There were a lot of senior citizens in that club. Think about the value of that. These were older people who were living on fixed incomes and who had a limited amount of dollars allocated to their entertainment. And they chose to go to Rutgers to watch these girls play. They could have done anything they wanted. They could have hopped on a bus and gone to Atlantic City—which maybe they did—gone to the church, or played a little bingo. But this was what they did, and they were faithful about it. Back in those days, we had two or three buses traveling to schools, such as Maryland, Providence, and Penn State, among many others. If there was an away game, you could best be sure there was a bus trip to it. Consider this: people paid their money to come, and they never had to worry about watching a game where our kids didn't show up.

And we had fun doing it.

My best teams always had a sense of humor.

When June and the twins were juniors, we won a tournament at Dartmouth. We went to the tournament banquet the first night in Hanover, New Hampshire, and my team decided it would be a great gesture to serenade the other teams with their singing voices. Army and Navy had just allowed women into their academies, and they were the other teams in the tournament, along with the Dartmouth, the home team. June, Chris Dailey, and the rest of the players decided to get up and sing "The Army Goes Rolling Along" and "Anchors Aweigh." They were pretty good, but as I had told them many times, "If you are going to draw attention to yourselves, you'd better be able to back it up."

"No problem, Therese, we learned from you," was their response.

Between the games, they knocked on the door of my hotel room and said, "'Come on, Therese—they always called me by my first name—we're going sledding." They had gone to the Five and Dime in Hanover, and they'd bought blue plastic toboggans with whatever money they had. They never had much. Then, they went out behind the hotel and went sledding.

They wanted me to go too because I wasn't that much older than they were. I thought they were out of their minds. I was sitting in front of this little fireplace in our hotel, and Jennie Hall came into the lobby. She was covered with snow from head to toe. I thought, these kids are going to kill themselves. Before the tournament, Joanne Burke had an injured leg. When I found out Joanne was out there sledding, I told her, "Don't even try to tell me you are hurt and can't play."

Joanne played very well.

That was who they were; they just wanted to have fun.

After the championship game, I just wanted to go home. Then, I turned around and saw a reporter who thought he was interviewing Patty, the MVP of the tournament. Only, it was Mary. You couldn't tell them apart. He certainly couldn't.

During the interview, he said, "Patty, you made all these shots. You played great. What do you attribute your success to?"

Mary, posing as Patty, says, "Oh, that's easy. Mary, my twin sister. She's our point guard. She got me the ball. She made some great passes. She is such a great player."

I turned and looked at Mary. I could tell them apart by their voices. The guy had no idea who he was talking to. This went on for about two and a half minutes.

Finally, the guy finished and said, "Thanks, Patty."

"Okay," I said to Mary. "What are you doing?"

"He didn't know the difference," Mary replied. "Besides, Patty won the MVP. And I got a little pub."

Mary could really handle the ball. We were playing Penn State, and Mary jammed her right hand pretty badly. She came out, and I couldn't even look at it. But she was tough. She went back into the game and played left-handed. We won, and she never had another turnover.

Another time, we were playing Maryland with Debbie Lytle, another Philly kid who had been the best player in the Public League. Mary decided she was going to take a charge against Debbie. Debbie knocked her flat. Finally, Mary got up. When she came out, our trainer, Sue Layton, asked her, "Mary, where did you get hurt?"

"Right there at half court," Mary said.

There was the time we played University of Maryland at Madison Square Garden over Christmas break. Their warm-up jackets looked just like ours. Maryann Deady, one of our subs, somehow wound up with one of Maryland's warm-up jackets. The regular season game with Maryland was at Rutgers that year. June, Chris, and the twins found a dummy and dressed it in the Maryland jacket and placed it on our bench. Chris Weller, the Maryland coach, was dumbfounded, not to mention, not pleased. Then, our president, Ed Bloustein, who loved our team, decided to sit on our bench for that game. Of course, he had to sit right next to the dummy in the warm-up outfit.

One time, when we were playing the early game of a double header, I saw one of our players, Patty Delehanty, running down the sidelines on the opposite side. Coming toward her was a woman in a red velvet blazer with a box of two pretzels, two hot dogs with mustard, and two Cokes. I stood there watching this. There was Patty—running, running, running—and this woman was oblivious. She was getting ready to watch the men's game.

Suddenly, boom! There was a huge collision.

Our players on the bench had towels over their heads because they didn't want the fans seeing them laughing. I couldn't laugh. The box went up. The cokes went up. The hot dogs went up. This poor woman had mustard dripping off her glasses. It was a scream.

When my teams get back together, they never talk about the games. They talk about the things that happened, the relationships, the conversations, and the moments that made them a team.

After one game, June was being interviewed in the training room after she had been selected to the Kodak All-American team. Our tiny locker room was just down the hall. The school had put a case of Coke and a box of chocolate bars in there for the players to eat. Patty Delehanty (nicknamed "LadyBug") came in and put a six-pack of Coke in her gym bag and was ready to walk off. One of the twins said, "Hey, yo, Bug, you can't take the whole thing." LadyBug took a can and threw it at her.

Meanwhile, June was still in the training room, and the reporter interviewing her asked, "How do you guys get along?"

"Oh," June said, "We're great friends."

And her teammates were in the middle of a huge cat fight.

In the meantime, I was recruiting Kristen Foley, one of the best prospects in the country. She came in and saw the whole thing.

June came back and said, "What's wrong with you guys?"

Bug got mad, threw down the Cokes, and off they went.

Chris Dailey was in there, and said, "You know, Bug, you've got to put those Cokes back."

Patty Delehanty didn't talk to June or Chris. This was bad because the three of them lived together. This went on and on. Finally, I approached June and Chris—the co-captains—and said, "Well, you've got to do something."

Chris said, "You know, Theresa, the longer this goes on, the easier it gets."

"Well," I said, "You folks have to fix this."

They eventually worked things out. But, to this day, they never bring it up—and they all go on vacations together. When June's father died, Bug was there.

One day, Patty Delehanty got into it again—this time, with our six foot, three inch center, Terry Dorner. They were banging the living daylights out of each other. I said, "Everybody in a circle. Now."

Chris was on my right and June was on my left. As I approached the circle, I thought, What am I going to do with these kids? Well, what did you do in first grade? Made them all laugh. So, I said, "This is ridiculous. We're a team, and we're fighting. You two are trying to punch each other's lights out. That's it. For the rest of the practice, we're going to hold each other's hands." Well, June lost it. Mary and Patty were both laughing hysterically. Here's the thing. Patty Delehanty and Terry knew what they caused, so they ran over and grabbed each other's hands.

We were able to break up a very tense moment with laughter. This, to me, was another essential lesson learned—the necessity of laughter to diffuse tense situations.

Any time you put more than two personalities together, there will be conflict, drama, call it what you like.

Put twelve women, girls together, there is bound to be drama. But teams need to avoid drama. It is self-destructive and self-defeating.

When we got together for the thirtieth anniversary of our first National Title at Immaculata in 2001, Cathy Rush made an interesting comment. She said, "Thirty years doesn't make a difference. People who were peacemakers thirty years ago are still peacemakers today. Drama queens will be drama queens thirty years from now."

Still, there were days when I felt I needed to be a psychologist. I wish I had studied it in college.

I was a no-nonsense, straightforward coach. When I was coaching, I was focused on one thing and one thing only: Winning. I didn't have time for other concerns. Our players ran our summer camp, and they taught the things I had taught all year. They were confident; and, by learning to teach, they learned the skills to play that much better. They knew what to expect.

We almost got to the National Tournament when June and the twins were freshmen in 1979, but we lost to Tennessee in the AIAW regional semifinals in New York. The next year, we advanced to the Final Eight and then ran into Old Dominion. I thought we finally had enough to win it all in 1981—after Kris Kirchner, a six foot, three inch All-American center from Maryland transferred in for her senior year, giving us a dominant presence in the post. We were so talented that year with Kris, June, the twins, Patty Delehanty, Chris Dailey, Terry Dorner, and Joanne Burke, a five foot, ten inch transfer from St. Joseph's who was a finalist for the Wade Trophy Award.

We got as high as number two in the country.

And, once again, life showed me to expect the unexpected. I was reminded that I might always be in charge, but I was never in control. Midway through the season, June—who was considered one of the ten best players in the country before the season—injured her knee cap in a game against Manhattan and was through for the season. We lost to Long Beach State by four points in the regional semi-finals in California. Our season was finished with a record of 27-5.

It seemed like we were always one player short. We just couldn't break through the glass ceiling. After that game, I wasn't angry at the team. I was just angry at life. I thought every time we get close, this happens to me. I was really mad at God. I know I was curt and short with the kids. To this day, I feel bad about that.

That spring, we had a recruit visit. I took her on a tour of the campus, including the dorms. I asked June and Patty Delehanty if they would show her their room. As we walked in, June and Patty were both sitting on their beds. I asked them to give the spiel about Rutgers. I proceeded, as I'd always done, to look at all the paraphernalia and posters in their room. I learned a lot about my players that way. I learned about their music, about their taste in art.

I noticed this one piece of loose-leaf paper hanging on the wall. It was a poem called "Footprints," and it was handwritten in pencil. It's the story of a young man, but they had crossed out "young man" and replaced it with "our young coach." The poem talked about a young man walking on the beach with our Lord and seeing two sets of footprints in the sand.

When the man reviewed his life, he noticed there was only one set of footsteps during the most difficult times. I'm thinking this is me all over again.

I thought, Well, this is interesting, and I continued to read the poem. In the next verse, the young man asked the Lord why there weren't two sets of prints because "You always said if I followed You, You would always be there."

The poem ends this way:

"The Lord answered, 'My precious, precious child, I would never leave you in times of struggle. When you see only one set of footprints, it was then that I carried you."

After I read that final paragraph, I felt like I'd been hit by a two by four. I realized I had been a real jerk. I had been so intent on reading this that I had no idea what was going on behind me. When I turned around, it was no longer just Patty and June in the room. The whole team had come in to join them—and me. They'd known I was coming.

I looked at all of them.

They didn't say a word.

They just looked at me.

I looked at them.

Okay, message sent. Message received.

CHAPTER 5

Finally, a Championship Ring

It's us against the world.

It may be hard to believe, but our 1982 Rutgers women's basketball team was the only program to win a National Championship since the university began playing intercollegiate sports in 1869. We won the AIAW National Tournament, defeating Texas, 83-75, at the Palestra in Philadelphia.

Our win came ten years after Immaculata had won the first AIAW championship in 1972, making Immaculata the first school to win the championship, and Rutgers the last.

When I'd come to Rutgers six years earlier, I had predicted this would happen. Once we won, the question was, how did we do this? The answer was simple: because of the team's work ethic.

It's nice to belong to an elite club, even if there was a little controversy attached. We had taken a lot of criticism all year for deciding to play in the AIAW instead of the NCAA tournament, where seventeen of the country's top twenty teams participated. But we had made a commitment to play in the AIAW the year before, and I wasn't about to let anyone label us second-class citizens. I didn't want anyone telling these players what they won wasn't worth something. Because it was worth a lot.

This team worked very hard to reach its goal. We won twenty-five games, and in the title game, beat a Texas team that had won thirty-two straight games. We had played all four teams that were in the NCAA Final Four, beating two of them—Cheyney State and Tennessee. We played eventual champion Louisiana Tech at Madison Square Garden in a close 83-73 game but lost.

The 1982 team may not have been as talented as our 1981 team, but they became the best version of themselves in March. The secret to all great teams is focus, chemistry, unselfishness, and love. We displayed those qualities throughout that season. We had six seniors—Mary and Patty Coyle, June Olkowski, forwards Chris Dailey and Patty Delehanty, and center Terry Dorner—all of whom wanted to go out on top—as champions.

And they achieved their goal.

Aside from the twins and June, the other two starters were Terry Dorner and Jennie Hall, a junior wing from Norristown, Pennsylvania. Our rotation included Chris, Bug, and a wild—but talented—freshman guard, Lorrie Lawrence. The roster also included another junior, forward Carol Glutz, and three other freshmen—Mary Pat Nespoli, Debbie Paladino, and Krystal Canaday.

Jennie Hall gave us that little pop of athleticism we needed at her position. Terry was very strong. She was from just outside Williamsport, Pennsylvania, and had gone to Mercer Community College, where she became a junior college All-American. When I visited Howie Landa, my coaching guru, he told me, "I'd always keep one eye on her." I thought, Okay, I see what I need here.

Terry was so strong. When she went into the gym to lift weights, the football players would clear out because she could lift a soda machine. Once she had established her position in the post, nobody was moving her. And she was fundamentally sound. Howie worked with her the same way he had worked with me. She had done a great job developing her low post moves when she'd work his camps. Her footwork then was so much better than most kids today. Throw her the ball, and it was an automatic field goal. Terry finished her senior year by scoring 626 points.

• • •

I always encouraged my players, and June was the living proof of the wisdom of that philosophy.

Whenever we had new students come to college, their first struggles were always about allocating their time, trying to accomplish all the things they had to do—training table, practice, conditioning, study hall, and classes. Their classes were from eight in the morning until five at night, so they had to deal with scheduling and time management.

People claim they are hard workers.

I was never too impressed with hard workers. I wanted competitors. A competitor never thinks about working harder. She just does it and gets the job done. Hard workers, on the other hand, will always work and do their job. However, that doesn't make a hard worker a competitor. Working hard all the time just becomes work, and then you get these ubiquitous words, "burned out." Basketball should never become hard work. It's a game, a game to be played with passion and joy.

"The very pleasures in life men acquire through difficulty." St. Augustine said that. So, you must work hard to gain the pleasure.

That's what happens today. So many people think, I'm great. I'm going to play this game, and that game. I'm playing well. But they can't understand why they can't get better. To them, everything is the same; same moves, nothing new to show off, each game is equal. You need to measure yourself. And you can't be afraid to find out you've come up short. Don't let anybody make excuses for you and your work. If it's not good enough, find a way to get better. I think you have to fail before you succeed. It will mean so much more to you when you have stayed the course and fought the good fight, and found a way to become successful.

June was a competitor. I've always thought that competitors were born, not made. Talent is something with which you are endowed. It is given to you. Your responsibility is to develop that talent. Skills are produced from developing talent. If someone says you have great potential, it means you have talent, but it needs development. The key to success here is very simple: hard work and perseverance to develop your skills will take you to the levels of greatness you seek. Good players do not become great because they don't want to spend time and put in effort to master their skills. In today's culture, people expect someone to hand them success. The idea of entitlement can deprive very talented individuals from the success they deserve because they were unable to put their signature on their work and spend the time needed to develop their individual skills. Young players today need to be able to handle the ball. There is only one way you can learn that skill, and it simply takes hard work and time.

Nurture talent and use it to your advantage—and that of your team. Talent works hand-in-hand with self-discipline. If a player has the one, she most likely has the other. Together, they combine to make a great player.

June had talent to the nth degree.

The greatest thing about our younger players was that they did not want to disappoint the juniors and seniors. A sense of accountability arose. They had to be responsible for their actions on the floor because they wanted to make a contribution. They wanted to be part of the group—the team.

There was never any frustration. As players, we always had that will to win. As a coach, my best teams felt the same way. I never thought we were going to lose. Karl used to say, "Theresa, you are such a pain. You think you can beat the Knicks."

I did.

I knew that the 1981-82 team had the potential to be special during our first exhibition game. We played the People's Republic of China's National Team in an exhibition at the Rutgers Athletic Center. They had a big girl on their roster who was nearly seven feet. You could put her in the doorway, and she'd block all the light coming through. We lost, 97-73, but we played well. Later, I told them, "Don't worry about that score. We're going to have a great year."

There was just something about them. You could feel it. They played for the joy of playing. They had dignity and grace. They had the will to win. I loved coaching them, and I loved watching them play. They were entertaining and selfless.

When we went on the road, our players may not have looked like they were walking out of Lord and Taylor, but they always looked nice. Our motto was,

"As long as it's clean, and bought, and paid for." Remember the Izod shirts with the little alligators on them? The twins couldn't afford the polos, so they bought two alligator pins and put them on their shirts. "Hey, Therese," they said. "We got Izod shirts."

When you played the twins, you played for keeps. They didn't just stand around shooting before practice. They always wanted to play one-on-one or taps. And they always played for Cokes. You always played for something. They never doubted themselves. I told them, "We're going to run these plays, and we'll use this defensive set. Let's go." You didn't have to twist their arms to convince them. They just did it, and it worked.

The media noticed us quickly. We actually played in the first college basketball game at the Meadowlands—pre-Bruce—and beat UCLA and their great Olympian, Jackie Joiner, 91-69. The men played the second game of the doubleheader against the Bruins, and they won, too. The next day, newspapers all over the country wrote about both teams. That was heady stuff for us.

Fans were interested in us, too, and our attendance grew.

We had great shooters. I had three one-thousand-point scorers on that team—Patty Delehanty, June Olkowski, and Patty Coyle. Because of their insistence on making only great shots, we scored eighty or more points in each of our four AIAW tournament games. We could run. And we could finish plays. The difference between a 60-60 game and a 60-48 game is one team outscoring the other by three points during every eight-minute stretch. We'd come down on a break, go through the legs, flip it the other way for layups. We always finished. Taking care of the ball was a prerequisite of this team.

Everything was running smoothly until the middle of the season. We were ranked third in the country. Then, June reinjured her right knee when she fell just two minutes into the game during our 68-57 victory over Tennessee on Saturday, January 24, 1982, at the Rutgers Athletic Center. June actually heard the knee pop in practice the day before the game. It was weak, but she iced it and taped it heavily. She started but didn't finish. (Knee injuries and their treatment have come a long way since the '80s.)

Terry Dorner picked up the slack with eighteen points and sixteen rebounds that day.

But the celebration was tempered by the fact that I thought we might not have June, who was a finalist for the Wade Trophy, which is given to the nation's most outstanding female basketball player, for the rest of the season. It almost happened. June missed four games, tried to play the next five, but was unable to contribute much. Then, she finally underwent arthroscopic surgery, missing another five games. We were just about to start our journey through the AIAW tournament when June came to my office. She was still hurting, and she didn't know what to do. She was in pain. She was second-guessing her decision not to have an operation her junior year and was wondering whether she should have gotten one now.

I told her she should put on her uniform and give it a try, so she did.

When she first came back against Georgia Southern and Minnesota in the four-team East Regional at the RAC, she was out of shape. Her timing was off and so was her shot. Eventually, she regained her confidence and played a huge role in our championship run in her hometown. Being a competitor is not always about winning and losing. It's about being able to handle the situation you are dealt. If you lose or are faced with an injury, you can't get upset because you've got to go back and face your demons—with determination and single-mindedness of purpose. That is how a player improves and becomes the best version of herself. You must measure yourself against the trials and tribulations that come your direction. Only then will you know the inner strength that you've been blessed with. The difficulties of life will show you the way to greatness and happiness.

The 1982 AIAW Final Four was held at the Palestra, where I had played in two Philadelphia Catholic League championship games when I was at Cardinal O'Hara. The old gym, opened in 1928, is a national treasure. But it had the hardest rims in the world. This was before they had roll-out basket stanchions. The backboards hung on top of a pole that was embedded into the floor. When I played there in high school, the place was sold out—9,200 kids, most of them screaming students who rode to the games on buses.

This time, it was one huge roar for thirty-two minutes.

I was coming home. And so were the twins, June, and Jennie Hall, who grew up in Norristown, just outside the city. My Philly connection. It was all good.

I still remember traveling from New Brunswick to Philadelphia to play Villanova in the National Semi-finals. We were stopped at a traffic light. All of a sudden, a woman started banging on the front door of our bus. I got out of the bus and spoke with her. She needed a ride to Crozier Medical Center to be with her sick child. I asked our driver to make a slight detour. Some things are more important than basketball.

We got by the Wildcats the next night, 83-75.

Don't tell anyone, but when I was at Immaculata, I had Villanova men's basketball season tickets.

The game had a local rivalry feeling to it because we had four starters with Philly roots who had chosen to leave the city. On the way into the building, a security guard stopped June and told her, "You should have gone to a Big Five school."

"We still hear that all the time," June said.

"I guess the people here feel cheated we didn't stay and play so they could watch us four more years. It's a lot like what Gene Banks did when he left West Philly High to play for Duke—on a much smaller scale," Patty Coyle said.

Although the crowd was just 1,879, we had to scrap the entire game. Villanova was good. They were 28-3, had a six foot, four inch center, Lisa Ortlip, a terrific guard, Nancy Bernhardt, and two hard-working forwards, Kathie Beisel and Stephanie Vanderslice. Villanova came into the game with a fifteen-game winning streak. They had beaten us earlier that month in the EAIAW seeding tournament and had a 34-27 lead at half.

I was hot. Just before half, I wanted Patty Coyle to make a pass to June. She didn't make the pass. They were on the other end of the court. At halftime, I was mad as hell. I stormed out onto the floor and headed right toward Patty. I was in her grill. "That ball goes inside. Do you understand?"

She wanted to say, "Therese, back off. It's okay." But Patty thought better of it.

June and Jennie Hall eased my mind. June made a pair of three-point plays and stuck four jump shots as we erased a 49-47 deficit and roared to a 61-51 lead. And Jennie came up huge against a school from the Philadelphia Main Line that was just five miles from her home. She made all eight field goals she'd attempted and was eight-for-eight from the line for twenty-four points. Thank goodness.

June finished with eighteen points in twenty-five minutes. And Terry Dorner outscored the wiry Ortlip, 21-13.

"When you win, it doesn't hurt," June claimed. "When you lose, you need all the painkillers you can get."

That team never really worried about game plans or scouting reports. They worried more about what they had to do. Sometimes, as coaches, we spend all our time on scouting reports, but I felt if we just executed, we'd be fine. We had players who were very skilled with the ball and were deceptive with their passing. They created an illusion of quickness, and they could beat a much more athletic team because their skill level was off the charts.

We needed all that and more when we played Texas.

The night before the game, Mary was so nervous, she left our hotel and took a trolley back to her old neighborhood and played with the boys at Finnegan playground for two hours for a little extra competition. The day of the game, there was a shoot-around. Texas came in. They had these expensive warm-ups on, flesh-colored tape. I took my team out the back door and said, "I'll see you back at the hotel later tonight." My kids were down at 33rd St. on the Penn campus, buying cheese steaks, sitting on the curb. Patty Coyle said, "I know we're going to win this game. Don't know how we're going to win this game, but we're going to win this game."

This was not a game for the faint of heart.

Before the game ever started, there was a little personal drama. Karl Justin was not in his seat. He had made a new friend. He was having his picture taken on the lap of the Texas Longhorn mascot. Good photo. Bad Boy.

Patty scored thirty points, shot twelve-for-thirteen, and was having the game of her life. She was voted MVP of the tournament. But that didn't stop her sister from screaming at her. Patty got yelled at all weekend. Mary played eighty minutes of almost flawless basketball at point guard. Normally, I'd give her a breather. But Lorrie Lawrence, our other point guard, had been suspended for violating a team rule, so I was out of options. I went to Mary and told her, "Don't look over at me to come out of the game because I'm not taking you out."

I saw how important this was to the twins and to everybody else just by looking out on the court and seeing the determined looks on their faces.

Terry Dorner had twenty-five points and twelve rebounds, dominating the paint. Jennie Hall had sixteen points and nine rebounds. We played the matchup with a half-court trap and were doing okay with it. Chris Dailey was playing out of her mind and directing the match-up defense beautifully. But, still, we couldn't pull away.

At one point, I called a timeout. June said, "I can't make a shot." She was zero-for-ten at that point. Chris Dailey, one of her best friends, called her out. "We can see that," she said. "Now, please, get some rebounds."

With the score tied 59-59, Patty scored six straight points. Then, Terry got an offensive rebound she had no business getting. She just reached back, got the rebound, and went back up and scored to send us up eight. Texas got thirty points from the great All-American, Annette Smith, and wouldn't go away.

The Longhorns fought back repeatedly and looked like they might catch a break when Terry Dorner fouled out with 3:13 to play. They cut the lead to 77-75 with 2:22 to play. Then, June gave us all a glimpse of the great player I had recruited. She made an off-balance jumper, and then made an incredible, over-the-head pass to Patty Coyle for a layup to help us pull away.

I brought all six seniors to the press conference with me. The first thing the media wanted to know about was June's pass. Before I could answer, June jumped in with her own interpretation. "Oh," she said. "We work on that all the time in practice."

It was good to see her smile again.

I didn't want to think that this was the seniors' final game. I didn't want it to end, but I was excited for them to go forward because I knew they'd be successful. I wanted to see how their lives would turn out. I wanted them to walk in their greatness.

When we cut down the nets after the game, Fred Gruninger was there, along with Eddie Bloustein.

"Well, I guess this means you'll want rings now?"

Yes, that's exactly what this meant.

All I could remember was our first championship at Immaculata. We thought we would get rings. Instead, the nuns gave us rosaries. So Rene, Maureen, and I had rings made. It was a diamond chip in the center of a basketball. When Mary and Patty were in high school, they were always asking me if they could try it on.

Now, each could wear her own.

And so could I.

It was so nice to hear the big bell in the Old Queens Tower ring when we got back to campus. I swear, you could hear the sound of it from Philadelphia through New York City.

The reaction even touched the late Sonny Werblin, a Rutgers graduate and a huge fan. He founded the Jets and had an office in Madison Square Garden. After we won, he wrote me a letter. "I never in all my days thought I'd be writing to a woman, congratulating her on being Number One at Rutgers," it read.

We got the girls to autograph a basketball for him, and I arranged to give it to him at his office. He asked me to come to the Garden to have lunch. So, I hopped on the train and got there early. I wore a suit and heels. I waited outside the restaurant at the top of the arena. I guess it opened at noon, and I was early. Anyway, all the men were coming in, and I was still sitting outside. Finally, one guy came out and said, "Can I help you?" I guess it was annoying everyone on the wait staff that I was sitting there. I said I was waiting for Mr. Werblin.

He looked at me funny, went off, made a call, and must have found out who I was. The next thing I knew, he ushered me into the restaurant to this special table and offered me a drink. The best thing was that one waiter came by and brought me a telephone in case I needed to call anyone while I was waiting. I called my secretary, Henrietta, and told her I had nothing to say, but I'd always wanted to use a phone in a restaurant. Everyone else in the restaurant was wondering who was this woman who was sitting at Sonny Werblin's table by herself, waiting for Mr. Werblin.

We had a wonderful lunch. His son later told me he kept that basketball prominently displayed in his office until he died. The spoils of victory are sweet.

At the team banquet, June and Chris got up to speak and couldn't resist presenting me with two gifts—a bottle of aspirin and a dime.

"You'll need the aspirin when you try to teach next year's team the match-up zone," Chris said.

"And you'll need the dime to call us if you need help," June added.

Pictures

THERESA SHANK SHOOTING HER CLASSIC JUMP SHOT
IN A GAME HELD AT ALUMNAE HALL.

PLAYING BEFORE A PACKED HOUSE AT VILLANOVA UNIVERSITY
AGAINST EAST STROUDSBURG STATE COLLEGE.

NET CUTTING CELEBRATION AT THE PALESTRA IN 1982 AFTER RUTGERS WON THE AIAW NATIONAL CHAMPIONSHIP GAME.

TEAM PHOTO FOLLOWING THE 1982 CHAMPIONSHIP GAME.

THE PRESS CONFERENCE AFTER THE 1982 CHAMPIONSHIP GAME. THERE ARE QUITE A FEW FUTURE DIVISION I AND WNBA COACHES SITTING AT THAT TABLE.

KATHLEEN TELLING ME WHAT I NEEDED TO HEAR, NOT NECESSARILY WHAT WANTED TO HEAR.

KEVIN AND MYSELF CUTTING THE NET DOWN AFTER
AN ATLANTIC 10 CHAMPIONSHIP.

PAT HEAD SUMMITT, THERESA SHANK GRENTZ, BETTY JAYNES, BETH BASS, AND JODY CONRADT AT A CELEBRATION FOR WOMEN'S BASKETBALL.

AFTER A VICTORY IN THE NCAA REGIONALS HUGGING MY SON, KARL.

THE 1990 GOLD-MEDAL WORLD CHAMPIONSHIP CELEBRATION IN MALAYSIA.

THE 1990 GOLD-MEDAL GOOD WILL GAMES COACHING STAFF IN
SEATTLE, WASHINGTON. FROM LEFT TO RIGHT, LIN DUNN, THERESA
SHANK GRENTZ, JIM FOSTER, AND LINDA HARGROVE.

Theresa Grentz, 1992 U.S.A. Olympic Women's Basketball Coach.

SUZIE MCCONNELL-SERIO AND MYSELF DURING THE 1992 SUMMER OLYMPICS IN BARCELONA, SPAIN. WE WON THE BRONZE MEDAL.

COACHING ON THE SIDELINES AT ASSEMBLY HALL IN CHAMPAIGN, ILLINOIS.

FAMILY PHOTO AT THE 2001 WOMEN'S BASKETBALL HALL OF FAME INDUCTION. FROM LEFT TO RIGHT, KARL, KEVIN, BRIAN (MY GODSON), MYSELF, KARL JUSTIN, AND KATHLEEN (BRIAN'S MOTHER AND MY FORMER ASSISTANT COACH).

A FUN PHOTO WITH MY TWO FAVORITE GUYS, KARL JUSTIN, LEFT, AND KEVIN, RIGHT.

KATIE HAYEK AND MYSELF AT A MOVIE SCREENING OF THE MIGHTY MACS.

JUST SOME OLYMPIC FRIENDS! FROM LEFT TO RIGHT, NELL FORTNER, BILLIE MOORE, MYSELF, PAT SUMMITT, AND VAN CHANCELLOR.

CHAPTER 6

Rutgers' Revival

*You can't get your second wind
unless you use your first.*

The challenge in coaching does not come with winning the first championship.

It comes in defending it.

I knew that from my days at Cardinal O'Hara High School and Immaculata.

After winning the first one, you have only so much time to enjoy it. Then, you have to let it go. That's why it is hard to create and sustain a dynasty. That's why you have to give Pat Summitt of Tennessee and Geno Auriemma of UConn credit for what they've accomplished. They've built dynasties. Of course, they have great players, and that makes it a lot easier. But you have to go get them.

I thought we had recruited a really good group to replace our six seniors. But it never quite worked out.

That group hated the fact that I constantly brought up players from that 1982 team. "We don't want to hear about Mary, Patty, Chris, and June." I felt that until you give me something else to talk about, it's not going to change.

We finally got it back on track in 1986 with two special players—Sue Wicks and Kristen Foley. As a coach, you are always searching for the one perfect player. I came close. I found two excellent players. Sue was a force of nature—the best player I ever coached in college. Kristen was a born leader. Together, they brought us back to national prominence.

Sue Wicks came along at the right time for me. She enrolled in 1985 and blossomed in 1986. She was a three-time Kodak All-American who led us to appearances in two NCAA Elite Eights and one Sweet Sixteen from 1986 through 1988.

Sue grew up in Center Moriches on Long Island. Her father was a commercial fisherman. She was kind, generous, and athletic beyond words. Sue learned how to compete at a young age, playing soccer and football with her brothers over the objections of her mother who constantly yelled at her, "Susan be a girl. Why would you want to do that?"

Sound familiar?

As soon as her mother went back in the house, the games would start up again. They always ended in a fight.

Eventually, the guys got too big and strong. Sue turned to basketball. She was consumed by the game. She would play before the school bus came, at lunchtime at school, then practice with the girl's team before working out with the boy's team.

Again, sound like anyone we know?

By the time she was a senior, she had grown to six feet, two inches and was almost unstoppable, averaging 39.6 points a game. She went off for fifty-nine points in a game against Longwood High, making her first twenty-five shots and punctuated her performance with an eye-popping dunk. "Sue could score fifty points a game if she wanted to," her coach, Dietmar Trick, told *Newsday* in 1984. That was enough to grab my attention.

I had no idea how far her hometown was from our campus until the day Chris Dailey, who was now my assistant, and I drove out to watch her play in an open gym. First, I had to go watch her play soccer. She was a goalie on the team. The turf was so soft my heels sank into it. After the game, she made her way over to the auxiliary gym to warm up for an intra-squad scrimmage. All I remember was her repeatedly jumping up and grabbing the rim. Then, she went downstairs and tore up the scrimmage. I used to call the teammates on her high school team "The Cabbage Patch Kids." The point guard was a kid with every kind of band: headband, wristband, armband, elbow band, and leg band. She cracked me up! Sue would bring the ball down the floor and then hand her the ball and get into position. "Now, wait. Wait, Wait. Now, throw it to me," Sue would say. Then, she would make the play.

We beat out over one hundred schools for her signature on a National Letter of Intent.

That was the easy part.

I'd like to tell you Sue made an easy transition to college ball. She had great one-on-one skills, but no idea how to run an offense. I'm sure it must have been frustrating. Midway through her freshman year, she wasn't even sure college was for her. She went home. Her father, who wanted her to get a college degree, took her out on the ocean in his fishing boat for three days in January.

Then, he called me.

"She's ready to come back," he said.

"Well, we'll be more than happy to take her back," I told him.

Sue's career took off from there. She led our team to the first of nine consecutive NCAA appearances in 1986 and was the National Player of the Year her senior year in 1988. Sue was inducted into the Women's Basketball Hall of Fame in 2013, and I can still remember her acceptance speech.

"I couldn't remember the plays," she said. "It was kind of a joke. One-play Rutgers. The joke in the locker rooms of the other teams was that 'You guys at Rutgers have only one play because you can't remember the plays.' And I said, 'The joke in our locker room is, you can't stop it.'"

The big difference between that team and my 1982 team was the fact that I was a little older now. I loved scrimmaging with the 1982 team, but I was too old to play with the team in '87. Sue actually ended my career. We were down at St. Joseph's, and I went up to take a shot, and Sue came out of nowhere and blocked it. I thought, Well, that's it. I'm officially retired.

Sue could do that to you. She holds records at Rutgers for points scored (2,655), rebounds (1,357), scoring average (21.2 points per game), rebounding average (10.9 rebounds per game), field goals made (1,091) and attempted (2,099), free throws made (473) and attempted (641), and blocked shots (293).

The scoring and rebounding totals are records for a male or female player at Rutgers.

Sue, who had grown an inch, and six foot, two-inch forward Regina Howard were our two inside powerhouses. Like Sue, Regina struggled at first with her adjustment to college. She was so homesick her first week on campus that her mother drove down from Albany to stay with her in the dorms. After a week of this, I told her Regina was going to be fine, and it was okay for her to go home.

That was just a temporary glitch in a stellar career. In my mind, Regina was always going to be a great player. I was coaching Rutgers in a road game at St. John's when a guy came up to me. He gave me a program, and he wrote on it, "Here's a name you should check out." Any tips I got, I checked out. I went out to Long Island to watch Regina play and, after three minutes, I called our equipment room and asked what numbers were still available. I went back into the gym, and after the game, I said to her, "You're going to play for me at Rutgers, and I won't take 'no' for an answer." That day, she signed with us.

When Regina came in, she was raw. I put a trash can near the baseline and said, "Regina, you're going to dribble a ball around that trash can five hundred times and then take the ball to the basket." She figured out how to do it. She could get to the basket in one move. Then we taught her how to throw the ball on a back door cut over her ear to a cutting teammate. It took time to learn. But I could see what she could become.

In time, Regina became the other half of the "Wicks and Sticks" combination and finished as the third leading scorer in school history.

Kristen, our fifth-year senior forward, was the brains of the operation.

In addition, we had two very good sophomore guards in Janet Malouf and Telicher Austin.

Janet grew up in Milltown, New Jersey, and played point guard for St. Peter's High School near campus. She started attending my basketball camps when she was in seventh grade. She was a point guard. She idolized Patty and Mary, who were counselors there and were like her big sisters. The counselors always played against the campers, and it was a great relationship back then. Janet dreamed of following in their footsteps and becoming part of the next version of the Rutgers Lady Knights.

Telicher was from Paterson Eastside in North Jersey, and she averaged twenty points a game her senior year in 1989. I loved how she was built: physically strong. She could take a beating as well as give one out. And she had great hands. That combination is deadly in women's basketball.

Coaching that team was easy because it flowed. The fans loved them. I can remember Janet missed a couple of games with a sprained ankle. When she walked back out onto the court for warm-ups, she received a standing ovation before the game had even started.

Some years, in coaching, it's like pulling a truck. When you have those years, you're trying everything you can think of to get your team to the last game of the season. Other years, it is so easy that you are just along for the ride. You're flying on their coat tails. And, when your kids all start pulling in the same direction, it is as easy as breathing. I used to tell my teams, "You never stay the same. You either get better or worse."

Those two teams in '86 and '87 were destined for greatness. They didn't need a whole lot of attention. You pushed them, challenged them in practice. And they performed.

I can remember Pat Summitt's father once saying, "If you're going to the Kentucky Derby, you don't take a mule. You take a thoroughbred." We had thoroughbreds.

And they were motivated. They wanted to be good. They had goals. All of my best players and best teams did. And they never doubted what I said.

Today, kids doubt everything.

That was a special team. It had everything—talent, unselfishness, and loyalty.

Especially loyalty.

Kristen Foley was our captain.

We had recruited her in 1983. She was a national prospect from Peabody, Massachusetts, and she epitomized the characteristics I was looking for in a player. She was one of those special recruits coaches dream about.

When I knew we would lose six seniors from our National Championship team in 1982, she was the first player I went after. Kristen was a five foot, ten-inch forward. I first spotted her at a summer camp run by Mike Flynn in the Poconos. She was clearly one of the best high school players in the country.

Folks in New England are very taciturn to begin with, so you don't know if you're winning or losing in recruiting. I just kept proceeding, sent a lot of personal notes, talked to her. I went to a lot of her games. I flew to Boston. Do you remember the plane that landed short of the runway at Logan Airport and wound up in the back bay? I flew over that area all the time.

Kristen was the type of kid you wanted to watch play. Sometimes, recruiting was not so much fun. I had this two-headed dime. Heads, I didn't have to go. Tails, I didn't go. Sue Wicks, who was selected National Player of the Year when she played for us in 1987, was the same way. She lived all the way up in Long Island, but I couldn't wait to get into the car and see her play. There were some kids I loved watching play: the twins and June, Kristen and Sue. I could sit there all day and watch them play. I just enjoyed what they did and how they played the game.

I went to their graduations. I sat there, watched them leave high school, and thought, Okay. Now, they're mine.

Kristen and I hit it off immediately. She was excited about coming to Rutgers. Later, she told me her mother wasn't so sure about her leaving New England to go to school in New Jersey. I needed to show her family that I would take care of her, so I made a special trip to her high school graduation. When I went to the house, Kristen modeled her prom dress for me, so I figured things were going to be all right.

Then, the weather sealed the deal.

Peabody held its graduation outdoors. As luck would have it, the day Kristen was to receive her diploma, it poured rain. The wind was gusting. But I'd promised Kristen I would attend. She told me when her mother saw me sitting in the audience, getting soaking wet, she knew everything would be all right.

I thought she was a good fit for us.

I loved recruiting smart kids. You looked out on the floor, and you knew whether they were smart or not. You could tell by the way they presented themselves, the way they handled themselves. They all had that same upbringing: good childhood, strong parents. The anchors were there. The values were there. Kristen was like that.

Kristen had the makings of a star.

But she tore up her ACL as a sophomore. I was there when she was operated on. Originally, she wasn't going to have surgery. But, the first time she tried to play, she went down trying to play the 1-3-1. Then, we realized we had to do something. First, though, she had to find the right doctor. She was operated on in Philadelphia, and her mother stayed at my mother's house for the week.

Every time one of them went down, I thought, How can I help them? In the hospital, I was there when they went to sleep, and I was there when they woke up. That was my motto: "When it hurts them, it hurts me." I hated to see the parents go through it with their child. That was very hard. After all, they wanted the best for their child.

They put her in a cast from her hip to her ankle.

Eventually, Kristen came back to become a three-year starter and someone I trusted implicitly. Kristen was reserved, but she was all business—a natural leader. They say leaders aren't born. They're made. But some people have certain instincts that come out at the right time. You just have to develop them. And she was loyal to a fault.

The players nicknamed her "Elmer," for Elmer's Glue, because she held the team together.

Just before the start of the 1986 season, Kristen had earned a trip home for the weekend because of her pre-season work ethic in practice. The entire team knew how much Kristen was looking forward to seeing her family. But I also knew responsibility is realizing it's not about you alone. It's about others.

That Friday, I waited for her at the bottom of the stairs at the RAC before practice. I spoke to her about her plans for the weekend. I never said she should pass up her trip home, but I mentioned we would be practicing Saturday, and we would be without our captain. Kristen just listened.

The next day, when the team gathered for practice, Kristen was with us. All the players knew the personal sacrifice she had made. It set the tone for the season.

If Kristen hadn't done that, I don't know where that team or my career would have gone.

As it turned out, we won twenty-seven games, were ranked in the Top 10, and advanced to the regional final against Old Dominion. And I got to celebrate the birth of my second son, Kevin.

I got to see St. John's Hall of Fame coach Lou Carnesecca recently. Back in the day, when the NCAA selection committee announced the teams for the tournament, they didn't have the selection show. The committee would be given a contact number to call. When I was at Rutgers, it was my number they called. I had a little more of a coaching voice, a raspy voice, back then. The Penn State student paper even labeled me and my voice, "The Rod Stewart of women's basketball."

I got the call, found out who we were playing, where we were playing. Then, I called the athletic director, and his son answered the phone.

I said, "Hello. Is Fred Gruninger there?"

And the kid said, "Hey, Dad, it's Louie Carnesecca."

Fred jumped on the phone, all excited. "Hey, Coach, what's happening?"

"No, Fred," I said. "It's Theresa Grentz."

"Oh."

It was like the air went out of the balloon.

I was excited, though. We were officially back on the national map, advancing all the way to the Elite Eight before losing to Old Dominion.

The next year, in 1987, we went 30-3 and were ranked as high as second, in the country. We didn't lose at home again and both Sue and Regina reached an important milestone.

Regina was a year older than Sue, and they were very good friends. In fact, they both scored their one-thousandth career point in the same game—against West Virginia in 1987. Sue was going to reach that milestone the night of that game, so I told the officials to be prepared. She needed only thirteen points, and I had ordered a dozen roses to give to her. Regina needed twenty-eight.

Sue reached the goal quickly, and we presented her with the roses. She went into the stands and handed them to her mother, along with the game ball. Then, she got back onto the court.

Meanwhile, Regina was playing like a woman possessed. She was flying down the floor, getting easy layups, flying back, getting a steal. She was on a rampage. Finally, I realized what was going on. I asked my assistants how many points she had scored at that point.

They told me she had twenty-eight. I sent one of my managers into the stands to get the flowers back from Mrs. Wicks. I used the same roses for Regina. They split the roses that night. The next day, I ordered another dozen. They split them, too. Now, just for fun's sake, can you imagine me going to the opposing coach before the game, and telling her Sue Wicks needs thirteen points to score one thousand, and, oh, by the way, I have another player who needs only twenty-eight to do the same? You wouldn't mind stopping the game for her, too, would you? This is "what not to do" in Coaching 101!

We won the Atlantic 10 title that March and advanced to the NCAA East Regional final again where we played top-ranked Texas for the right to go to the Final Four. We might have gotten there, too, if Ellen Bayer, their six foot, ten-inch center, hadn't played. Before the game, she couldn't find her shoes. Mimi Griffin, of ESPN, went and found her some. We played Texas down to the wire and lost an eight-point heartbreaker to the team that eventually completed a perfect season by winning the National Championship. Both Kristen and Sue made the All-Region team.

I realized this group of players was more than a team. It was a family.

I place a high value on loyalty. I wanted—I needed—a staff I could trust to have my back and who was able to recruit the players who could play for me. Loyalty is a key piece of a successful team. And if it spills over into your personal life, so much the better. If you don't have loyalty in your life, you are in a ship all by yourself, out on the sea without a rudder. As a coach without the loyalty of your team, you find yourself thinking one thing, while the team is in the locker room, saying something completely different.

That's really tough.

I've said before that I never wanted a whipping boy on my team, even though there was always a player less talented than others, and perhaps a little different from the rest of the group. I expected the more talented player to help her struggling teammate. The ability to reach out and be aware of the surroundings of your constituents and being able to offer solutions is the sign of a respectful leader. The mature players who demonstrated these unselfish qualities were the foundation of our championship teams. I told my players we could fix any problem, as long as we worked together and were honest with each other. When the best players in the program bought in to the system, everything else fell into place. The opportunity to observe and watch the young women under my tutelage grow and become women, great women, I considered a privilege, and one of the best joys of my profession.

A loyal player is someone who really cares about her teammate and says, "Okay, I'm going to help you out here." When someone does that for you, and you know she went out of her way to help you, you're going to make darn straight that you're not going to disappoint her. Playing basketball is a task. Learning to be unselfish, responsible, and trustworthy is an art. Playing sports gives you the opportunities to learn such qualities.

And that's exactly what they did.

I think about this all the time. Kristen had that team in the palm of her hand: Regina Howard, Sue Wicks, Telicher Austin, and Janet Malouf. If she said jump, it was how high, when, and where? She had them right where she wanted them, and they responded.

Some people live by the idea that their self-worth is determined by whether they win or lose the game. But your self-worth is determined by how you do things. And how you treat others. That's a component of leadership. You must be a model for others.

To me, it all goes back to the military.

There are rules. Everybody has rules.

I was never in the military, but I loved it. I loved the idea of an honor code. I read all the books I could get. I used to visit West Point. Kristen's uncle was a general in the Vietnam War. I asked Kristen to ask her uncle to recommend several books on leadership that I should read. He recommended books like *Command Decision* by Kent Roberts Greenfield, about twenty-three crucial decisions in World War II, and Sun Tzu's *Art of War*, a treatise on military strategy, attributed to a legendary Chinese general. They're still on my bookshelves today. I read them and learned a lot. Basically, I learned that it's how you react to those rules that determine your leadership potential.

During Kristen's final two years, we were unbeaten at home. Losing was not a part of that team's vocabulary. Besides, I thought losing was the dumbest thing in the world.

But I remember we had one game in which we weren't playing very well. We were losing. I called timeout, and I got all over one of my younger players.

"You have got to play tenacious on defense," I told her.

The team went back onto the floor, and Kristen, my stoic captain, was out there laughing.

I called her over. I was confused. "Do you want to clue me in on what's so funny out there?"

"Therese, I don't know how to break this to you," she said. "Your freshman wants to know what number is tenacious."

I asked the assistants, "What's the number of the opposing player she is supposed to be playing?"

They told me, and, in my best Philadelphia accent, I said, "Hey. Yo. Twenty-two."

We finally pulled the game out. When we were in the locker room, the kid put her arm around me—nobody touches me—and said, "What did you think?"

"I'll tell you," I said. "Nobody's played tenacious like you did tonight."

Later, I told my staff, "We've got to work on our scouting reports. Let's start by working on language skills."

My best leaders all led differently because of their personalities. But they all had the same characteristics—work ethic, a trustworthy nature, responsibility, courage, respect. They all had respect for people who could not do much for them. How do you treat people who can't do anything for you? A lot of people blow them off, saying, "What good are you?" until they find out what they can do for them. I was never like that. I didn't care if you were the president and lived in the main hall or you swept the floor—because I'd done that. I swept the floor in high school every day. At the end of the week, I got one dollar from our coach, Maryann Nespoli, which I then exchanged for tokens to buy a drink at lunchtime.

Aside from Kristen, I had a number of good leaders at Rutgers like Chris Dailey, Sue Wicks, Regina Howard, Vicky Picott, Amy Reynders, and Cheryl Cop. The list goes on. Our leaders were very aware of everything. They were so in tune with the group. They had the pulse of everybody on the team: how they were feeling, how their day was going. They had the capability to assist their teammates, to help them succeed. They were always giving, serving. They had enough self-confidence to be leaders. They knew that basketball wasn't focused just on them. It was on the entire team.

One for all and all for one.

That was something we taught. We must have done something right because a lot of my former players found their way into coaching. I measure my success by succession.

I was amazed. Why do these kids want to get into this profession? Get a job. Do something. Muffet from St. Joseph's, Mary, Patty, June, Chris, and Jennie Hall, all from my championship team, all got into coaching. So did Kristen, Sue Wicks, Janet Malouf, Missy Lender, and Vicky Picott. Six players from my 1997 Sweet Sixteen team at Illinois—Krista Reinking, Melissa Parker, Kelly Bond, Ashley Berggren, Aimee Smith, and Bonny Apsey—all followed suit.

I was at the Final Four a couple of years ago, and three of my former players were there. Muffet was coaching Notre Dame, Chris was the associate head coach at UConn, and Kelly Bond was an assistant head coach at Texas A&M.

But they are teachers first. They are not just coaches. I think that's what's made them exceptional. When I look back over my career, the teams that had the kids who went into coaching were the successful teams. Those kids truly loved the game. They understood the game, whereas a lot of kids play the game because they have to play the game.

They also knew what I was looking for in a player.

I hired Kristen as one of my assistants when I was at Rutgers. One time, we were recruiting one of the best players in the country. We were fortunate enough to get a home visit. Kristen went with me to sell Rutgers basketball. We were ready to sit down when the family dog showed up. The girl we were recruiting just shooed her away. The dog scampered away, whimpering.

I knew then what my assistants didn't.

I kept the conversation short. We left.

When we got into the car and were driving back to campus, Kristen asked me what was up.

"You know, Kris, I don't know," I told her. "If she treats her dog that way, how is she going to treat her teammates? I'm not so sure she should be in a Lady Knight uniform."

That was that. We didn't recruit her.

At the beginning of the 2013-14 basketball season, I was humbled and honored to receive the Joe Lapchick Character Award—along with Nike global executive, George Raveling, and the late Don Haskins, who coached Texas Western to its historic 1966 NCAA Tournament win—at the New York Athletic Club. What made this award so special was that it was named after the late Joe Lapchick, who was a Naismith Hall of Fame member and a great ambassador of the game. He had coached St. John's and the Knicks in the '50s and '60s. Lapchick was a role model who exemplified the qualities of honesty, humility, loyalty, integrity, and unselfishness.

Because the award speaks to character, I could have asked any number of my former players to introduce me.

But I chose Kristen Foley.

Enough said.

Those teams helped build the Rutgers brand. Hubie Brown once said, whenever he coached a team, he would make sure they stayed in the best hotels. They were going to look the part, act the part. I remember thinking that there was a lot to that. When he would go to practice, he would wear matching coaching shirts and pants. No gray baggy sweat suits. I thought, If that's what the men were doing, that was what we should do, too.

I remember my rules—you had to come in looking like you were the coach. A professional look at all times.

I had a certain dress code for our staff and our players. If you played for Rutgers or went to my camp, you had to wear Rutgers gear. If someone wore another team's shirt, I'd make her tape over the logo. The only exceptions were a Team USA shirt or a shirt from your alma mater. I remember when I first started coaching we would budget so much money so I could buy a couple of suits that I would rotate throughout the twenty-seven games of the season.

Eventually, I turned into a clotheshorse on game days.

And I loved every minute of it.

One time, when we were playing West Virginia, I had a gorgeous tweed suit on, shoes to match, and a little tie—very Annie Hall. Well, something happened in the game, set me off, so I whipped the tie off. Then, off came the suit jacket. One of their fans yelled, "Hey, Coach, what are you going to take off next?" Then, their pep band started playing the theme song from the movie *The Stripper*. I thought, Oh, my gosh, I'd better keep my clothes on. So, I did. And that was the end of that.

In retrospect, I was tough on the 1987 team because I knew they had so much potential. I was talking to my former Rutgers assistant, Kathleen, and said to her, "I almost feel like I should apologize. I was so curt and so tough on them. I read some of the things I wrote to them. I wasn't mean or degrading, just short and to the point."

"Oh, no," Kathleen replied. "They are all better women because of what you did."

Live and learn.

But it reminds me of a story about Vince Lombardi. Like him, I tried to go to Mass every day. I enjoyed listening to the homilies. There were several priests during my coaching career who were excellent homilists. I'd absorb their lessons and try to pass them onto the team. Vince's son wrote a book, explaining what it took to be number one in your field. In it, he said his father went to Mass every morning. In reply, his quarterback, Bart Starr, said that Coach Lombardi needed to go to Mass every morning because of what he did on the football field every afternoon.

Kids need discipline. And that's why I really have no desire to coach anymore. Here's why. One day last summer, I had a teaching lesson with three boys, two seventh graders and an eighth grader. Loved them. I asked them to do something and told them how I wanted it done.

I asked them three times, and they didn't do it.

Then, I shifted into my old coaching voice. They stopped in their tracks and looked at me. I realized what I had done. And I stopped. "Oh, oh, that doesn't come out very often. That's just Coach Grentz. It's okay. It's all right."

I thought I had put that part of my personality to bed. When I was coaching, it was out there all the time. I learned how to be very comfortable living outside of my comfort zone.

Sue looked like she was in her comfort zone when she was invited to the 1988 Olympic trials. The Olympics were her dream come true, and she was at the top of her game. She always considered herself to be confident, steadfast, and goal-oriented. Then, she walked away from training camp. "I had an anxiety attack," she said. "I didn't know what it was. I didn't know what was happening. I was so young. I didn't know to ask for help."

Olympic coach Kay Yow reached out to her in an attempt to alleviate the situation. But Sue didn't take advantage of her offer.

"I couldn't forgive myself that I wasn't stronger," Sue said. "I closed the door on myself."

She didn't forget, however. The experience served as motivation for her professional career, which sent her from the Mideast to Asia with multiple stops in Europe. "The Olympic experience taught me to think—this is what you love to do. You don't want to lose it," Sue said. "Your reputation as a pro is on the line."

Before the establishment of the WNBA in 1997, American female athletes hoping to pursue a career in professional basketball had to go overseas. During her senior season at Rutgers, representatives from professional teams in Japan and Italy came to visit Sue with the hopes of signing her to a contract.

She signed her first contract on a napkin, deciding to play in Lake Como, Italy. It initially was a struggle. "The first year it was miserable trying to learn Italian and being away from the nurturing, sheltered environment that I had at Rutgers," Sue said. "The fans, because they loved their home team so much, had to hate you as much. They had chants where they would call me names and throw stuff at me."

Eventually, Sue embraced her new lifestyle. She loved the challenge of being in a new culture and playing a different style of basketball.

She left Italy after three seasons and headed to Japan, where she became immersed in "the perfect culture for team basketball," in which her team practiced from noon to 6:00 p.m. daily. She stayed on the move, playing in Israel, Spain, France, Turkey, and Hungary.

After ten years as a professional overseas, Sue got the call that would bring her back home—the WNBA had been formed. With the thirtieth overall pick in the inaugural draft, the Liberty picked her. Sue played six years and made the All Star team in 2000 before retiring in 2003.

Sue coached for a while, including at her alma mater, Rutgers. But now she's part of a business called Fight 2B Fit, a youth-fitness program that works with schools and other organizations in the New York area. Sue talks about how inner-city children, in particular, face many obstacles in establishing physically healthy lifestyles. Schools have cut back on physical education, and many kids have very little in the way of even safe spaces to play outside.

"When I was a kid in the summer, it was out of the house at eight in the morning, and don't come back until lunch," Sue said. She is now forty-six. "And don't come home again until dinner. Other than that, we were outside all day. We created our own games. Kids need to move; they need to play or else they act out in different ways. Once you stop moving, that becomes a bad habit."

My time at Rutgers was filled with unforgettable players like Vicky Picott, who came to us from nearby Hightstown, New Jersey, in 1988. She was one of the most recruited players in the country. She came because she said, "How could I not go where Sue Wicks and Regina Howard had been?" She was an incredible player, a four-year starter. She still ranks fourth in school history in career points (1,792), third in rebounds (1,029), and fifth in steals (225). Vicky was named the Atlantic-10 Freshman of the Year and was an All-Atlantic 10 selection three straight years. We beat Georgia to win the Bell Atlantic

Tournament at the Garden one year in a game we had no right winning, and she was unstoppable. She went off for thirty-five points. She played overseas for eight years, and then eventually got into coaching when she returned to the States. She is currently an assistant at Vanderbilt.

There was my 1994 team, which created a major earthquake. We were small, 9-3, unranked, and at a crossroads when we played Tennessee, which was 14-0 and ranked number one, in a game at the RAC on January 17. The morning of the game, we were wrapping up shoot around. We were circled around half court, and out of nowhere, a bird flew from the rafters and landed on the Rutgers logo on the sideline just off of half court. I said, "Well, ladies, guess what? That is a very good sign."

We were hoping for a sellout crowd to be the sixth man. Unfortunately, a blizzard came to town, shutting down the entire state of New Jersey. A little over eighteen hundred people braved the elements and came to that game. They were the loudest eighteen hundred people I've ever heard. They were a very successful sixth man. January 17 also happened to be the due date for my assistant, Kathleen. I told her to stay home because I didn't want her out in the blizzard pregnant. I told my brother, Chuck, Kathleen's husband, to make sure she stayed home. Neither one listened to me! Chuck pulled his truck right up to the back door of the RAC, and in wobbles Kathleen just as the game was about to begin. I gave her strict orders to sit behind the bench because you never knew what could happen on the bench—balls could fly, players could bump into you. It was unpredictable. But that didn't last long. Why listen to me? I'm just the head coach. Kathleen roamed back and forth from the water cooler to the scorer's table, tapping me on the shoulder any time she had a suggestions. And her suggestions were very fortuitous.

The Lady Vols, coached by Pat Summitt, had superior talent. But we found a way to win the game with basically five and a half kids, largely on the efforts of Caroline DeRoose, a six-foot forward from Ghent, Belgium. We ran the Princeton offense and we backdoored them all night. She finished with thirty-five points, which tied the school record for points in a game that was originally set by Patty Delehanty against Pitt, back in 1982. Caroline had a huge night, making ten of thirteen shots, including five of five from three-point range. She was ten-for-eleven from the line and played the entire forty minutes.

We jumped out to a huge lead early, then held on by making ten straight free throws in the last two minutes. The media was calling it the upset of the decade. What I will always remember about the game was the fact that Caroline had her shorts on backward. That was back when you wore Champion gear, and you had a little "C" on the shorts. As Caroline was running down the floor, I asked my assistants if she had her shorts on backward because the "C" was in the back. When we went in at halftime, I told her, "Don't you dare change those shorts. Wear them just the way they are."

Like most coaches, I was superstitious.

Late in that game, Caroline came up to me. She looked exhausted. "Coachie," she said. She always called me Coachie. "Call a timeout."

I called a timeout. I asked her, "Why did I call this timeout?"

She said to me, "I just needed to breathe."

I told her, "Okay. Just sit down. I'll take it from here."

That's the type of relationship we had.

After the game, Pat Summitt and her assistant, Mickie DeMoss, came out of the locker room to see Kathleen and me. Pat said in her southern drawl, "Kathleen, after that game, you haven't had that baby yet!?" Brian Charles was born five days later on January 22.

We used that win against Tennessee as a springboard to get to my final NCAA tournament at Rutgers.

That 1994 team also included two guards—Cheryl Cop and Amy Reynders—who were excellent students.

One day, I noticed Cheryl did not look good, so we took her in for a physical. The tests came back, and the kid had juvenile diabetes. It was really hard. She got into games, and, by the end, she made these mistakes she ordinarily wouldn't have made. I told the doctor and my staff, "I need to know what the story is and how she's handling it." It turned out that the big muscles were eating up the insulin. A doctor came to our practices. He told me she was the most disciplined patient in his practice. I asked him how many other Division I point guards he had in his practice.

I was very careful with her. We always had orange juice. We always had practice at the same time because when you change a diabetic's schedule, it throws her off. Some days, she'd come in and say, "I'm going to be Coach Cop today," because she just couldn't practice.

When we played in the 1993 Atlantic 10 tournament, it was the year they had the big blizzard on the East Coast. Ron Bertovich, the commissioner of the league, wanted to move the game up from 3:00 p.m. to 11:00 a.m. I said to him, "Oh, no, we're not. There's going to be nobody here."

I finally told him Cheryl was a diabetic, and we'd scheduled everything according to the original schedule the conference gave us.

"You don't want to change game times at this time, trust me."

Long story short—we played it at 3:00 p.m. And we won.

Then, there was Amy Reynders, the epitome of a student-athlete who was a finalist for the Rhodes Scholarship and is now an ear, nose, and throat doctor in Rochester, New York, where she grew up. I remember visiting her at home. As soon as I saw the straight As on her high school transcript at Aquinas Academy, I knew she was headed for big things. And I wanted to be a part of that.

Amy was a three-year starter, a two-year captain, and the Big East Scholar Athlete of the Year. She had a brilliant college transcript in microbiology, too.

Whenever we were going through a rough patch, she took the time to write something inspirational to her teammates. Not everyone does that. Most of them just sat there with blank looks on their faces. "Okay, put something in me." But Amy was willing to share her emotions with her teammates. When you give of yourself, it comes back tenfold.

One semester, she was getting a B+ in organic chemistry. That sounds good, but I was afraid that grade would affect her chances for a post-graduate scholarship.

I went to our academic advisor and told him I needed a tutor for one of my players.

When I told him it was Amy, his initial response was, "She doesn't need a tutor. She has great grades."

I looked him square in the eye and told him she needed an A in this class for medical school. She received her tutor and got an A in the course. It was kind of interesting to me that we tutored weaker students to keep them eligible to play, but not the stronger ones, who were in search of something more than playing basketball.

We even changed our practice schedule to accommodate Amy's lab times on certain days.

Several years after Amy graduated, we met at a football game at Rutgers. I asked her what medical school was really like. "Coach," she said. "After you and basketball, medical school was a breeze."

Those were the kind of kids I had the privilege of coaching at Rutgers.

I would have stayed there forever but...

In 1992, after I got the Olympic coaching job, Fred Gruninger started talking about the future of sports in the '90s and the growth of corporate sponsorships. I talked with the late Dave Gavitt, the founder of the Big East, and David Stern, the commissioner of the NBA, and I could see where this was going. I called Joan Cronan, the AD at Tennessee and had a meeting with her. I also called Donna Lopiano of Texas. Both of these women were doing great things. They had highly successful programs that were drawing big crowds. I wanted to know what they had done and how I could do the same at Rutgers.

It took me eighteen months, but I did it. I had a plan. I wrote a proposal for what I thought we needed to do at Rutgers to keep our program competitive with the top women's programs. I took it to Gruninger, and he laughed at me.

I knew that he didn't really care about women's sports.

Right then, I decided I wasn't staying there. I wanted some corporate sponsorship and fundraising. I wanted to recruit fifteen donors to endow scholarships so we could move forward, be more competitive, and win championships.

I was so disheartened; I didn't go to the Final Four that year for the first time ever.

One day, when I got home, there was a phone call from Karol Kahrs, who was the senior women's administrator at Illinois. She told me the school was interested in talking to me about the coaching job there. At first, I told her I wasn't interested in Illinois. I was really thinking about quitting the profession for good. I prayed about it: "Look, Lord, if you really want me to coach, then help me out here."

Then, I decided maybe this phone call from Illinois was the sign. They say there are no coincidences in life; everything happens for a reason. When the call first came, I wanted to laugh. I wasn't going to Illinois, but yet, I knew I needed a change.

When I decided to leave, it was hard leaving my players. I still have a letter from Amy Reynders that she faxed to me before I accepted the job. There is no question that the relationships I built with those kids made it even harder to say it was over. The only thing I decided I wouldn't miss was cleaning that great big house. The boys and I used to do it every Saturday when Karl went to play golf. Then, one year, I gave up house cleaning for Lent. It was such a sacrifice. I never did it again. Amazing how that works!

No regrets. It was just time for me to go. My work at Rutgers was completed.

CHAPTER 7

Crisis Management

Always take responsibility.

M y coaching career was a lot like riding a roller coaster. There were some great high times, and there were some low times. Unfortunately, 1985 was one of those down times for me. Not only was I fed up with the way my teams were performing at Rutgers, but I had also started to doubt myself as a coach.

Then, I made a life-changing decision.

I accepted a job to coach the US Select team in the Jones Cup in Europe and Taiwan. The trip lasted from May 16 through July 2—fifty-two days. I left my husband and our eleven-year-old son, Karl Justin, home.

The trip was something I had to do.

One of my goals in life had been to coach the US Olympic team, and coaching a select team was one of the steps involved. I used that trip to reaffirm my beliefs. Chris Weller, the coach of Maryland who was my assistant on the trip, and Sandra Meadows, a high school coach from Texas, set up routes everywhere we went. We had training sessions, took walks at six in the morning, and did sprint work on the soccer fields when there were no gyms available.

It got to the point where the players called me "General Patton." But they loved it.

And so did I. I considered it a compliment.

Two weeks into the trip, I had called Karl twice. I had written lots of letter in between. After our talk, I went back to my room and thought, I can't come home with anything less than a gold medal. If I brought home anything less, I'd have been a failure because of the sacrifices he and I were making. I knew I had to work harder than I ever had before.

A lot of observers said this was not one of the stronger national teams ever to play overseas; and when we won the gold, I felt a sense of redemption.

I'd gotten my first taste of international basketball during the summer between my junior and senior years at Immaculata. I played for the United States in the World Championships in Russia. Now, I thought I was tall——always had, as a matter of fact. But, when I got over there and saw Russia's six foot, ten-inch center, Illyana Semonova, who was ten and a half inches taller than I was, this almost-six-footer felt like a Smurf in the land of the giants. She wore number six, and I barely reached the six on her jersey.

As you might have expected, Russia won the gold medal. The US won the silver. When they handed out the medals, they already had our names engraved on them. I guess they knew who was going to win the tournament. But it was a great learning experience.

I coached internationally for twelve years, from 1981 through 1992. I coached the Junior National Team with the great Cheryl Miller in 1981, coached the Jones Cup, and then went on to coach our World Championship team and Goodwill Games team in 1990. We won three gold medals. And I felt confident—in both my teams and in myself. I also found out how difficult it was to win away from the states.

These trips were hard. You were away from your family, your college program, and basically your whole routine. I used these trips to build my spiritual life, as well as my physical training. Shopping, fast food, and delicatessens were all a past memory. I had physically felt better after working out with my assistants. Truth be told, I also felt better after losing some weight due to food poisoning I contracted in Malaysia. After Malaysia, we headed to a week's R&R in Hawaii. (This was not be hard to take.) Our next trip would be to Seattle for the Goodwill Games.

Since I hadn't seen my boys in a long time, I'd asked Kathleen to bring them to Seattle. I don't know what I was thinking, asking my assistant coach to bring a twelve-year-old and a four-year-old across the country! When the three of them arrived in Seattle, I was waiting for them at the gate. The two boys ran right past me. Kathleen was about to walk past me, too, but I called out her name. They didn't recognize me because of all the weight I lost, or so they said. (I personally think they just forgot what I looked like.) Kathleen had to grab the boys and quickly point them in my direction, saying, "Kevin, Karl, there's your mom!" I was heartbroken they didn't recognize me, but after some hugs and kisses, we were all smiles.

Funny story about the Goodwill Games: After we had won the gold medal game, I waved to Kathleen to bring Kevin and Karl Justin onto the court because I wanted them to be a part of the medal ceremony. As Kathleen tells it, "I handed Kevin to you, and Karl climbed over the railing himself. After the ceremony, and after meeting with the press, Karl and I walked to the car. Kevin was with you, or so I thought." Somehow, after the press conference, Karl found his way back to Kathleen. I thought Kevin was with them. So, after all the post-game events and festivities were over, I left the arena and went to my car.

I saw Karl and Kathleen getting into their car and yelled over to make sure they had Kevin. Kathleen just stared at me, then screamed, "I thought you had Kevin!"

The look on our faces was one of sheer panic like you've never seen before when we realized we had lost Kevin.

I kept yelling at Kathleen, "I thought you had him!" as I sprinted straight toward the arena entrance.

She yelled back at me, "I handed him to you over the railing after the game!"

We were running all around the arena looking for Kevin. Kathleen found him with Nancy Darsch, the head coach of The Ohio State University at that time. When we reunited, a weight had been lifted off my shoulders. Any mother can relate to that terrible feeling of losing their child. As Kathleen put it, "At that moment, you were Kevin's mom and not Theresa Grentz, the head coach of the gold medal Team USA at the Goodwill Games. You were just a mom with your youngest son's arms around your neck." Indeed, I was Kevin's mom, Kevin's relieved mom, at that moment. What a day! I won the gold medal but lost my son. Kathleen was lucky she got to babysit again after that catastrophe. Thanks, Nancy, for finding him!

I'm convinced the reason we don't have world peace is because the whole world cheats. They all cheat. I was in Cuba. They changed the time left on the clock. I was in Yugoslavia. They changed the time. When I coached the Junior National Team, we played a preliminary round game. I rotated players in and out every seven minutes. Something didn't feel right. I asked my assistant, the late Fran Garman from LSU, to check the clock.

"Theresa," she said. "You have fourteen minutes."

I figured that couldn't be right. "I can't have fourteen minutes," I said to her. "I'm already on the third wave. Check it out."

She came back and said to me, "Well, now you've got sixteen minutes."

As it turned out, they just kept adding time because the US was winning.

At halftime, I told the team, "Listen. I can't tell you how long this second half is going to be, but if we lose the lead, the game is going to be over quickly."

We played in another town in Yugoslavia where they had a moon-shaped clock with a gate over it. I said to one of the officials, "I want to make sure that clock is working."

We were warming up. The next thing we knew, the clock stopped. I said to the officials, "If that clock is not fixed, we're not coming on the floor." We went into the locker room. They came to the door and assured me the clock was fixed. We came out. The clock stopped again. I pulled my players off the floor again.

When the game finally started, Janice Lawrence, my six foot, three-inch center from Louisiana Tech, got the opening tap; and, all of a sudden, the sprinkler system went off.

I guess we were too hot for them to handle.

The international trips gave me a deeper appreciation of history. Each city we played in seemed to have been a World War II battleground. In every city hall, there were pictures of citizens being hanged by the Nazis. I developed a new appreciation for the struggles that went on in the rest of the world that never touched our shores.

The experience gave me an up-close look at the price of freedom.

Playing for your country and dying for your country are two totally different things.

On September 10, 1990, I got the call I thought I'd always wanted.

A representative from USA basketball was on the phone, offering me the chance to coach the 1992 Olympic women's basketball team. Ironically, when I received what should have been one of the biggest honors of my career, I wasn't sure whether I wanted to do it. It took so much time. I'd be away for six weeks and ten weeks at a time. It would be hard on Karl and my two sons, Karl Justin and Kevin.

There is great pride in being named the Olympic coach. But, at that time, I didn't think it was my time to be the coach. I wished this honor had come much earlier or much later in my career. But we don't get to choose when we are called to do a job. I received many letters of congratulations and many bouquets of flowers, including one exorbitant basket from Nike. I remember standing in my living room and saying to Kathleen Shank, my assistant coach and sister-in-law, "I know this is supposed to be a very happy time. But it's almost like I'm watching my own funeral."

Lin Dunn, who was the Purdue coach, called and finally convinced me I couldn't withdraw.

"Okay, fine," I said. "But you have to be my assistant."

There was a lot of pressure involved in being the Olympic coach. I had to be sure I had the best team. And I certainly didn't want to lose. The team I took to Barcelona consisted of centers Daedra Charles and Tammy Jackson; forwards Teresa Edwards, Katrina McClain, Medina Dixon, Clarissa Davis, Vickie Orr, and Vicky Bullett; and guards Cynthia Cooper, Suzie McConnell, Carolyn Jones, and Teresa Weatherspoon. Six of them had played on the 1988 gold medal team. My assistants were Lin Dunn, Jim Foster of Vanderbilt, and Linda Hargrove of Wichita State.

It was a good team. They were elite players. I respected them for who they were, but I still expected things to be done the right way. Elite players are more focused. It's no nonsense. They were at the Olympics, and they knew what they had to do to win.

We had three players who were six foot, three inches. But I knew we were missing the one player my best Rutgers' teams had always had—a knockdown shooter.

We'd had one in Ruthie Bolden, the leading scorer on the 1991 World University Games team. But you wouldn't know it. She got hurt in training camp and couldn't play, suffering an injury that would later come back to haunt us.

I never thought there was any pressure on our team to win because everybody was following the men's Dream Team. We were an afterthought, in more ways than one. From the beginning, it was obvious the men were getting all the attention. I remember flying with them on the same charter jet to Monaco for an exhibition game. They had separated the luggage by colored tags. Blue for the men. Red for the women. We watched as all the men's luggage was collected, put on the bus, and driven away.

We stood there with our bags, waiting for our transportation. When it was obvious the bus was never coming, we picked up our luggage and walked out.

When we arrived in Spain, the scene was magical. Karl traveled with me and Aunt Kathleen and Uncle Chuck brought the two boys over to Spain. As everyone exited the airport and went to the top of the garage to pick up their rental cars, the Spanish military yelled at them to get down on the ground. They did. And they stayed down until the all-clear siren was issued. The military thought it was a car bomb; Kevin and Karl were never scared because they had no concept of international terrorism.

Welcome to Barca.

The Olympic Village was right on the water in this beautiful seaside city in the northern part of the country. I loved going to the cafeteria just to be around the incredibly dedicated athletes. To me, the Olympics had been about my watching these great athletic competitions that were held every four years and performed by the best in the world.

I was just inspired by being around the competitors.

It was a great experience, a once-in-a-lifetime experience. We were right there with Michael, Magic, and Larry, the greatest players in the world. Of the twelve players named to the US men's team, ten were named in 1996 among the Fifty Greatest Players in NBA History for the league's first fifty years. When USA Basketball held press conferences at the Olympic site, I discovered the power of the NBA. The men's and the women's teams were on the podium. There were three hundred media at the men's interviews, and maybe two or three for us.

I still remember them going to practice every day. Even the great ones need to work on their game. This was a very important lesson for me to learn and remember to pass on.

At least they got some time to themselves in the gym. Otherwise, it was just a circus. Players from opposing teams skipped their own warm-ups before games just so they could have their pictures taken with our players or get autographs. The US men won their preliminary round games by an average of forty-six points. Then, they blew out Croatia, 117-85, in the gold medal game. The team was so much better than the competition that Coach Chuck Daly didn't have to call a timeout the entire tournament.

But we had a world-class competitor, too—Teresa Edwards, the Hall of Fame guard. She was the real deal. She could play. She had a set of morals and principles. She never played in the WNBA. She played in the Olympics. She was fierce.

We had drills. We were doing competitive drill between the players and, naturally, keeping score. Something happened with the clock, and we didn't have the correct score. We decided to just move on. But Teresa came right back at me, saying, "Wait a minute. Who won this?"

Who won mattered to her.

Kids today don't make winning a priority. You go to a summer tournament, you play three games a day. If you win, you play at five. Lose, you play at seven. There's far more interest in getting exposure in front of college coaches than in winning a championship.

The men were totally supportive of us.

I coached one game, and I heard someone behind me screaming, "Give them hell, Coach T. Give them hell, Coach T." I couldn't turn around, but I recognized the voice. It was Magic Johnson. All those guys were right behind us all the time. I can still remember Karl Malone saying to me, "Now, anytime Utah comes to the Garden, and you want tickets for your sons, you just call me." You don't realize how large those guys were. Karl Malone's forearms were as big as most people's thighs.

My son, Kevin, who was six at the time, thought the Olympic competition was just another game. He didn't understand how big it was. But he was obsessed with getting Michael Jordan's autograph. He finally got it. Mission accomplished. I awoke one morning to read about him and his quest in Erma Bombeck's syndicated column in USA Today. No one knew how she got the story. But Kevin thought it was cool.

I really hoped we could duplicate what we all felt the Dream Team would accomplish and stand on the podium with them with gold medals draped around our necks. And, for a while, it looked as though we might. We rolled through the preliminary round games in our eight-team tournament, scoring 114 points—an Olympic record—against host team Spain. Medina Dixon and Cynthia Cooper were totally dominant.

Then, it all fell apart in our semi-final game against the Unified Team— what was left of the old Soviet Union.

The remnants of the former Soviet squad ran its deliberate offense while sitting back defensively in a matchup zone. And we couldn't hit a shot during a 79-73 loss. The game was tied 67-67 with 5:25 remaining, but they took control with a 6-0 scoring spurt. We shot just 35.8 percent (29-81 FGs) from the field and just 52.6 percent (10-19 FTs) from the foul line.

Medina Dixon finished with twelve points. Forward Teresa Edwards, the best competitor I ever coached, contributed eleven.

When I was a head coach, I knew two things: I was going to get the credit, and I was also going to get the blame. It was very important to teach this to the players. The coach sets up the game plan, puts it into action. Many times, I put the game plan in, and it worked beautifully. But there were times when it didn't.

The Olympics was one of those times.

There are three things people think they can do—bartend, start a fire, and coach. When you become a coach, everybody becomes a critic. Everybody knows what you should have done. It's so easy to coach from the stands.

After we lost and had a ten-minute cooling-off period in our locker room, it was time to face the media. I had to be able to explain and be accountable. I always thought this was important because sometimes coaches decide they don't want to talk to anyone after a disappointment. But you can't decide you are going to talk to people only after a win.

You're in it for both the good and the bad times. And you are responsible for both.

After we did the formal interviews, which were translated into several languages, I went back to the locker room to speak with more reporters. One New York radio guy said to me, "Coach, how will you deal with this for the rest of your life?"

My answer was this—and I had heard it twenty-five years before: "Some of God's greatest gifts are His refusals."

Then, he said, "Good luck in the bronze medal game against Cuba. We don't want to write this story again." Meaning, we don't want you to lose the game.

It was hard to lose, real hard. Inside, I was devastated by what had happened. I had never experienced anything like this in my life. I tried to tell myself there were ten-million Chinese people out there who couldn't care less. But I couldn't even do that because the Unified team was playing China for the gold medal.

That defeat almost killed me. I took full responsibility for our loss. I didn't act vengefully. I picked myself up and moved on, but it was very difficult. I was out there, pure and simple.

For years afterward, I couldn't go into a bookstore without buying a self-help book. I read every self-help book in the world. It was very difficult. I read six, seven books a week.

Karl is so good for me. He keeps things in perspective. When I retired, he said, "Theresa, we don't have your salary anymore, so please don't buy all those books." So, I went out and got a library card.

We came back to beat Cuba, 88-74, for the bronze medal. Teresa Edwards, the USA's first male or female to play in three Olympic basketball competitions, finished her storied Olympic career with eighteen points. We collected our medals, then flew home with the men's team. They were gracious. There was no celebrating on the plane because they knew how sad we were.

But I don't regret the experience. I learned to accept criticism, and that's not easy.

That loss changed the way USA basketball operates today. The women followed in the footsteps of the men's team, which went from college players to NBA stars in 1992. The women now conduct mini-camps prior to competitions. Their rosters are made up of professional players from the WNBA, making it a much better system.

What is positive about failing and learning from your mistakes?

Everyone who is successful has had their share of personal failures, a moment when things didn't go their way or as planned. What do they do? They evaluate situations, make corrections, and start again. You need to let go of disappointments. Learn from them, but don't dwell or linger on them. Move on.

Accepting all this was very important to me in the aftermath of the Olympics.

I realized I couldn't wallow in my mistakes. It's like acid. Acid destroys the container in which it is held because it eats away at it. If you are full of acid, you are rotting from the inside. When you love, it's from the heart.

There is a story of the Indian chief who told a brave, "You have two dogs inside of you—the good dog and the evil dog."

The brave asked, "Which one am I?"

The chief replied, "Which one do you feed?"

The choice is yours.

Afterward, when I thought about it, I realized how lucky I was.

How many people get a chance to coach an Olympic team? Here's this kid from Glenolden, Pennsylvania, who's been all over the world because of basketball. The red, white, and blue forever and forever. I still have my Olympic flag from '92. Whenever the Olympics are on TV, I fly the flag.

When I think about the Olympics, the experience will always be near and dear to my heart. But the disappointment always sticks with me as well.

In 2012, we were down the shore, watching the women's game, and my nephew said, "Aunt Theresa, the US is losing."

I said, "Oh, God, don't let them lose. Because if they lose, the name that's going to come up is mine because I was the last coach to have lost."

But that isn't true.

So many people today don't know if we won or we lost. They just assume we won.

That can be good or bad.

It's more of a personal thing. That loss is not something that's going to make me a lesser person. I had an opportunity to do something, and this is the way it turned out. The Soviet Union was breaking up. They might have needed a win more than we did. Who knows? I'm sure in my next life, I'll probably get a better answer. But, for now, I'm at peace with the outcome.

Even though I failed on the world stage, I realize there are many people with difficulties in their lives. The situations may be different, but all difficulties carry a weight of pain. My message is: you can get through it and live a happy life. It will happen. You just have to stay with it.

If only one person takes this message from my Olympic experience, it will be worth it to me.

And I would go through it all over again.

CHAPTER 8

Putting the Fight Back into the Illini

Sometimes a change is as good as a rest.

I was forty-two when I went to Illinois. Forty-two—still young and energetic. I had a chance to learn, grow, and figure out how to accomplish things, how to recover from failure and move on.

But, once there, I started aging quickly.

The program was a mess. It needed all the skills I'd learned so far—passion, loyalty, leadership, and even a little "car salesmen" mentality for it to succeed.

Case in point: the players would never wear their gear around campus because they were embarrassed to be seen in it. Illinois had suffered through eight straight losing seasons. It had finished last in the Big Ten the previous year. We were probably lower than dog biscuits on the food chain. We had one columnist out there, an older guy, who wrote a sexist column, suggesting women's basketball players were ugly and volleyball players were much prettier. Like that matters.

Volleyball was the big women's sport on campus before I got there. Eventually, that changed, but it took a while.

I hadn't realized how bad it was until I attended my first Big Ten coaches meeting. All my coaching colleagues were there. They acted very nice and polite, "Oh, Theresa, can we get you a sandwich, some coffee?"

"Yes, thank you," I said, thinking that's never happened before.

Well, I had never coached that bad a team before, either.

Then, I got to see the results from the coaches' preseason poll. We were picked to finish eleventh in the Big Ten. When my dad heard about it, he said, "Theresa, we weren't real crazy about your going to the Big Ten, but can you explain to me how you could be eleventh in the Big Ten?"

"Dad," I told him. "They have a unique way of counting out here in the Midwest."

I was so darn mad. I took winning and losing personally. I got up and walked out of the meeting. I drove back to Champaign from Indianapolis, all the way home on I-74. On the way, I called one of my assistants, Kathy McConnell, and told her to get the kids together for a meeting. Then, I told the players about how they were perceived.

Total silence, glazed looks. Finally, one of my players, guard Ann Henderson, who was in the back of the room, raised her hand and said, "Coach, you'll get used to it."

"No," I told her. "If we finish last, I'm going to kill you."

Two of the kids in the front row agreed. "I think she would," they said.

It was obvious. What this team needed was leadership—and from me.

To me, leadership has always meant service. What can I do for you to make you better? Leadership also means vision. It's important that the leader be someone who has a plan for success and who is willing to serve others in order to make that dream of success a reality.

Leadership is not just about barking orders. If you want to know who you are leading, turn around—see who's following you. If they are lined up behind you, ready to step into battle with you, then you are leading. And don't be surprised if sometimes you find that you can lead by walking behind them! There are times when I had to lead my teams by being first in line. And there were teams that I led by walking behind them.

When I was coaching, I thought about the power I had over my players and how I used it. I chose my words carefully. There is no question that young people remember all the unkind words spoken to them by people who are supposed to be—or are called—their leaders. Should you find yourself in a position to lead others, you must be intelligent, courageous, compassionate, and have trust in a being higher than yourself.

In addition, the leader needs to be willing to do whatever it takes to get the job done. Sometimes, that means cajoling or stroking a person. At other times, it may mean raising your voice to get excellence from the group. A common thread for any great leader is that her followers truly believe in that person and her leadership.

Leadership is influencing people. I needed those older, more experienced players to be a positive influence on the younger ones. I needed those older players to look after the younger ones in matters not just basketball but in life.

A leader has to be comfortable with herself and how she's lived her life, so when she kneels in front of her team and begins to tell them what to do, her credibility will stand up.

A leader must project calmness when faced with difficult situations. She has to project confidence. In coaching, you need to be able to say what you mean with clarity, which will be understood quickly by your team. In my case, this was often executed in timeouts. I think I loved these situations more than most. I loved it when we were playing a tough opponent, the game was on the line, and a decision had to be made. I enjoyed being in the center of the storm with my players. I loved guiding them to victory.

I tried to lead from the standpoint that, if for some reason I wasn't there, the group would carry on. To me, that kind of leadership is based on character, conviction, and compassion. Leaders need to be humble. You have to be able to share the spotlight and not worry about who's getting all the credit.

Being a leader can be lonely. If you are a leader, you can't be afraid to be alone with yourself. Decisions that I had to make, steps that I had to take, needed to come from me. I needed inner strength, and I looked to my God for that.

The players needed to know that they were good, that they could be competitive, and that they could win. I tried my best to convince them. They tried their best to win. Eventually, we succeeded.

But it took a while to change the cancerous culture. It had affected everyone, even Ashley Berggren, our best player. Ashley was a five foot, ten-inch sophomore guard, but she had great strength, like Sue Wicks. She was also kind of a loose cannon. At our second practice, I realized I was missing a player. As it turned out, Ashley had temporarily lost her mind. She got frustrated and walked out. The next day, she walked into my office to explain her behavior. "You know, Coach Grentz, I get very frustrated. I have a short temper, and when it blows, I walk out."

I told her I could understand that. I could see where that might happen. I said, "If you do that again, don't bother coming back because you're done. You have no self-control."

Later, the assistant coaches asked her if she saw me and asked what I'd said.

"She said if I ever do it again, not to come back."

My assistants looked at her and said, "Well, she meant it."

We never had that problem again. I found Ashley to be someone who really wanted to win.

Join the club.

• • •

I was fighting a culture of mediocrity at Illinois. And I was on a one-woman crusade to change it, starting with academics.

Being a basketball player and not being a good student was just unacceptable to me. I had come from a culture at St. Joseph's and Rutgers that valued academics. Our players at St. Joe's were all on the dean's list. In my nineteen years at Rutgers, our teams were ranked academically either first, second, or third among all thirty-two teams on campus. Many of our graduates went on to become doctors, lawyers, financial leaders, and head basketball coaches. When I asked one of them what made them so successful, I was told, "You taught us to call our own shots. So, that's what we did. No sense being vice president when you can be president."

At Illinois, my players told me their grades were high Cs. I told them Hi-C was a fruit drink, not a grade. My motto was, "Don't bring me any hooks."

One of my first requirements at Illinois was that my players attend all their classes. If you were not in your seat in class, I had a seat for you next to me on the bench.

That's rule number one.

It's always been my belief that when you enrolled in a class, you started with a C grade. The more you put into a course, the higher the grade. The less you put into a course, the lower the grade. Made perfect sense to me. I drilled this into my players from day one. "You will go to class. You will do your schoolwork. And we will win."

Simple, short, and sweet.

The second part of being a student is meeting all deadlines. I built a good relationship with the faculty, so I knew what was due when.

The same rules applied to practice. I expected my players to be on time, to be fifteen minutes early. No just running in at the last minute. It was Theresa Grentz time. We called it "Illini time." Then, the players started to hold one another accountable.

It all goes back to self-discipline. You have a job to do, do it. Do the right thing the first time. The way you handle things in your life will be reflected in your performance on the basketball court. If you are a half-baked student, you probably will be a half-baked player. Can we count on you to push yourself, even though at times it's inconvenient?

Obedience is something different. You join a team, and you believe in its goals, which means you must be willing to live by its code of conduct. It's a code of honor.

I have responsibilities to my team, too.

The rule I use is, if I teach you and you do not understand it, it's my fault. But, if I teach you, you understand it, and you do it wrong, it's your fault—and that's responsibility. Now, I have what I call my theory of twos. It takes me two minutes to teach you. It takes you two weeks to practice it. It takes you two months to become comfortable with it, to put it into a game.

I said to Karl the other night, "There are some kids I teach I think I could really coach. Others, I'd trade them. It all goes back to self-discipline and obedience."

He said, "What do you mean? They have to do things their own way."

That's not being obedient. If someone tells you to do something, you need to do it as well as you can under the instructions you are given, not just wing it. This is not the time to experiment. But there is a time to experiment. I never believed in putting fences around my players. Remember June and her backward over-the-head pass to Patty for a layup in the National Championship game with us up by four with just two minutes to play?

To me, that's a confident player. And that's what I wanted to instill in my Illinois team.

Some players bought in right away. Some took a little more convincing. Others, we just couldn't change.

We had a young team. When I arrived, I discovered I had no scholarships left to give out. So, I had to do the best I could with what I had inherited.

I knew our core group of sophomores—Ashley Berggren, Nicole Vasey, Krista Reinking, and Kelly Bond—were the future of the program. Ashley was our best overall player. Krista was our best shooter. Nicole was our best defensive player. Kelly was a point guard and also served as the emotional leader of our practice team. I took them out and told them they needed to take ownership of the team. It was a big ask, since there was very little, if any, positive reinforcement. We were playing in front of a near-empty arena, drawing maybe two hundred fans, if we were lucky.

"Most of the people there didn't know who we were," Krista said. "They were just the homeless trying to get out of the wind and the cold of Illinois."

I tried to upgrade attendance by starting a club called "First Game's On Me." I had a lot of speaking engagements and told the audience that if they came to a home game, I would buy them their tickets. It was an idea I borrowed from Jody Conradt of Texas, and it worked. The group sat right behind our bench and was loud in an attempt to make our crowds seem bigger and more enthusiastic.

Know the reason why you do something. Have your cause, and keep it in front of you.

I tried everything to keep their spirits up because I believed in them and wanted them to recognize that fact. I figured these kids had been through a lot. So, I started emailing them reflections every night. I addressed them as "Illini Women." I did this for almost a month and never heard a word. Then, I was out recruiting one night, got stuck, couldn't get back to campus and couldn't email the Illini Women.

The next morning, when I got back to my office, I had three players come up to me and say, "Where was our reflection last night?"

Kids are actually hungrier for these stories now than when I first started, and I'm happy to oblige because I've always been a storyteller. But it didn't save the season. We didn't finish eleventh in the Big Ten my first year. But we didn't win it either. We were 13-15. We finished seventh in the Big Ten and lost in the conference tournament in Indianapolis and didn't get to go to the NCAA's.

I vowed next year our season would not end in Indianapolis.

I came to Illinois to win championships. I kept repeating that to the players in practice. I made up signs—we will win. After a while, they began to think that either this woman really believed this or she is the nuttiest person ever to come to Champaign. I needed to convince my players that it would take just a little bit of effort on everybody's part, and we could do it. If you have a road full of potholes, and you try to fill them by yourself, it takes forever. But, if everybody helps, you can get it done quickly.

You just need to have some faith.

On Sundays, I attended mass. One Sunday, the priest was delivering the sermon of the mustard seed. In it, a man came to Jesus and begged him to heal his epileptic son. The father told Jesus he had tried to get help from the disciples, but that they had failed. Jesus ministered to the boy, and he was cured. When his disciples asked him why they were unable to do the job, he told them it was because of unbelief. He then proceeded to say, "If you have faith as a mustard seed, you will say to this mountain, 'Move from here to there,' and it will move; and nothing will be impossible."

Powerful words. And ones that had particular meaning for me.

When I came back to my office, I asked my secretary to get me a box of mustard seeds. She looked at me like I had lost my mind, but she did it. A mustard seed is very, very small. Then, I asked her to bring some index cards, and we glued one mustard seed to each card and put a player's name on each one.

The next day, I spoke to the team about the mustard seed and how much faith and trust they needed. I said this is all you need and gave them the cards. It must have struck a chord.

Little by little, we started winning the players over. At the end of the school year, the team got together and decided to work really hard in the summer and be accountable to each other. They got up at 7:00 a.m. every morning and ran or worked out to improve their skills and get in shape.

To inspire them, I talked to them about my days at Rutgers and my favorite players over the years.

"There was a set of twins called the Coyle sisters," Krista reminded me recently. "A lot of their opponents nicknamed them, "The Campbell Soup Kids." You always spoke so fondly of these people. It was easy to see how much you cared about them. I made my mind up that I wanted you to tell stories about me to the next generation of Illinois players."

Thank you, Krista. Your wish has come true.

Just before summer break, I held an end-of-the-year meeting with our players. Ashley came in and told me she wanted to become an All-American. When Ashley was in high school, she wanted to go to Duke, but they backed off at the end, and she had to decide between Illinois and Vermont the year before I arrived.

When she told me of her ambition, I was very calm. I never said that's a little out of your league. We came up with a plan. I told her this is what we have to do, and here's how we're going to do it. I never questioned her or doubted her resolve. I told her one of the things she had to do when she stepped on the floor was to be cocky. I told my players that all the time. You can be lovely on this side of the line. But, when you are on the court, you have to have an attitude. You've got to know you are good—and act like it. She started to realize how all the little things—coming to practice five minutes earlier to shoot free throws, staying late, helping someone else out—added up.

She used that as motivation.

Nicole Vasey had motivation of her own. She was actually a contestant in the Miss Illinois competition. She was as beautiful on the inside as she was on the outside. Her family said the rosary every day.

One day, when we were practicing, she missed a shot and blurted out an uncharacteristic, "Jesus Christ."

I said, "Nic, don't blame him. He didn't miss the shot."

"I was just asking for a little help," she replied.

Our practices were hard. But Nicole's dad was a Marine and told her what I was doing would eventually make her and the rest of the team better.

Sophomore year was a difficult one for Nicole. Her good friend, Eric, committed suicide, and she was devastated. She played a game and dedicated it to his memory. The next couple of weeks were difficult for her. Eventually, she recovered and became an important part of our success.

When it came time to putting together a coaching staff at Illinois, I tried bringing my sister-in-law, Kathleen, with me from Rutgers to be my top assistant coach at Illinois, but because she is married to my brother, Chuck, my mother did not want another one of her children to move away from the East Coast. So, my mom won out and Chuck, Kathleen, and baby Brian stayed in New Jersey. When I left Rutgers, Karl Justin was a junior in high school. My first year in Illinois, Karl Justin stayed with Aunt Kathleen and Uncle Chuck in New Jersey to finish his senior year in high school.

I had learned a very valuable lesson from Joe Reed, Renee Reed's dad. Renee was my assistant at Rutgers from 1993-95, then I brought her to Illinois with me. When Renee and her brother were in college, her dad would write to them every Monday. Joe was a former military person and a very successful businessman in finance. I valued his life experiences. Every Monday, I would hand-write Karl Justin a letter. Whatever money I had in my pocket, which usually wasn't very much, I would put into the envelope and send it off. After the first month of letters, young Karl mentioned to me how much he enjoyed them. He said to me, "Before you send the next letter, could you look in Dad's wallet first before sealing the envelope? Just a thought, Mom."

In addition to Kathy McConnell, who also came from Rutgers to Illinois with me, one of my first hires when I got to Illinois was LaVonda Wagner, who had been a member of the previous Illinois staff. I had observed LaVonda at multiple Final Four events and always thought she'd be an excellent addition on my staff. She'd been interviewing at Old Dominion and Stanford; she had zero interest in staying. After she agreed to meet me at my office, I had to ask her where it was. This was all so new to me. After a four-hour conversation, she agreed to stay. I never regretted that decision.

She knew the league and did a lot of my early scouting reports, which was extremely valuable in my first year. And the recruiting system she implemented for us was outstanding. She put everything in a book, information on all our prospects, itineraries for the month, organized it, and then went to Kinko's and had it bound. I was sitting at one event with Tara VanDerveer of Stanford and she asked me, "Where'd you get that?" I told her my staff did it. Next thing you know, Stanford is doing it. Early on, I said to LaVonda that we needed something to set us apart when we were recruiting kids in the summer. She came up with the idea of us wearing monogrammed coaching shirts— which were always ironed and starched—and using cuff links.

I had a vision of what this program should be. LaVonda once said to me, "We bought into it even though we did not understand most of it. There were days you were on planet Mars and the rest of us were just trying to catch up with you. When we had a meeting and you started to talk about dates, we always asked first, 'What year are you talking about?'"

In short, she was just what I needed.

The stage was set. Illinois was finally ready to take on the Big Ten.

CHAPTER 9

Bringing Back the Glory

Leadership is vision.

I had been right; all we needed was faith in ourselves.

The following year, in 1997, we won twenty-four games—the most victories in school history—and grabbed a piece of the school's first-ever Big Ten regular season championship.

We had set the tone for that season during a huge victory over Wisconsin at Madison. It was the second game of conference play. We had lost to Purdue in West Lafayette, Indiana, on a Friday. We'd had a three-point lead at half but then suffered a complete meltdown with seven minutes to play.

You know what kind of mood I was in. Not good. Not good at all.

We rode the bus up from West Lafayette to Madison for a Sunday game. I was so mad that when I got to my room, I found that someone had arranged for an exercise bike to be delivered, so I could work off the steam. (I wonder who that little elf was.)

I didn't want to eat with my team. I'd had meetings with the players all morning. "We're winning. Do you understand? We're winning."

Now, it was time for practice on Saturday morning.

I thought we were going to the arena in Wisconsin. This is the Big Ten. Instead, the bus pulled up to the Salvation Army building. My assistants were whispering in the back. Finally, LaVonda Wagner got up and said, "Theresa, this is where we're practicing."

Why? The arena was booked. There was a farm show going on there. So, I'm out because of cows and cheese. Terrific.

Then, she said to me, "Oh, yeah. One more thing. In order for us to practice here, you need two canned goods for us to get in." And she handed me two cans of string beans.

We went into practice. Now, the court was surrounded by paper towels and diapers, ready to be dispensed by the Salvation Army. I decided that I was going to work this team hard.

The next day, we went to the game. There were fourteen thousand people, a full house. Members of the Illini Club had arrived in buses. I thought, This is the Big Ten. This is big time. I was wearing a wool suit, with a silk camisole underneath, and snakeskin heels. By halftime, I was soaked.

We were up three again, just like the Purdue game, and I didn't want the roof to cave in on us again. I had just read Phil Jackson's book, *Sacred Hoops*, in which he writes about having his team do Zen exercises. I lined up the players, told them to close their eyes, and imagine us in victory. I opened mine because I wanted to see if any of the players were looking back at me. They weren't. They all had their eyes closed.

We took the court after halftime. Seven minutes to play and, sure enough, we started throwing the ball all over the place again. I waited. Then, I called timeout. I told my team they had just taken Wisconsin's best punch. Now, all they had to do was go back out, stand their ground, and finish this game. They went back out, stood their ground, and won the game. Later, I heard Ashley Berggren had held a meeting after a foul and told her teammates, "If you think I'm practicing with her all next week after losing two straight games, you are out of your minds."

I didn't know if it was my coaching or the garbage they didn't want to put up with that won us the game. And it didn't matter.

All I knew was that win ignited something in them. I was more than happy to provide another motivational spark for them the next week.

• • •

LaVonda would often drive me to my speaking engagements. In our car rides, I would ask her what she thought I should tell these people. I never had anything written down, and if I did, it was probably on a napkin. I know it drove LaVonda nuts, and she recently said to me that she would think, How does this woman think she's going to get up in front of an entire group of people and speak to them without anything prepared?

Sure enough, I would get up before the group, give the speech, and receive a standing ovation. Then, I'd get in the car, and we would go home. I always asked LaVonda how the speech was. (I always knew the speech was very good!)

LaVonda wanted to learn how to do this. So, I made a deal with her. I would teach her public speaking if she'd help me with my workout schedule. So, every morning, LaVonda would set up two exercise bicycles in front of a blackboard in The Huff. I would get on the bike and give LaVonda a topic to speak on. She would start speaking, and I would make comments like, "L, that's boring." "Who's your audience?" "What information are you giving these people?" "You have to engage this group, LaVonda." This went on for about six weeks, and I knew LaVonda was ready. She may have begged to differ, but I knew it was time for her to give it a try.

LaVonda was a special person and a great assistant. I called her one day telling her to go speak in my place at a little function. She did as she was told. When she arrived, she realized that this was not a little function; the place was large, and it was packed. In addition, the group was extremely disappointed that I was not there speaking. LaVonda was in the middle of a fire and had to think on her feet. "As you can see, I am not Theresa, as I do not look like Theresa. I am taller than Theresa," she told the large crowd. Interesting choice of words, considering LaVonda is an African-American woman. She lightened up the crowd, put them at ease, and never looked back. She was a hit!

Naturally, on the way back to the office, she was not happy with me and how I sent her out to this little function that turned out to be not so little. When she approached me about why I would do this to her, I very calmly looked at LaVonda and said, "If I had asked you to do the speaking engagement for me, would you have done it?"

"Absolutely not! I wasn't ready to speak in front of a big group."

I looked at LaVonda and said, "That's funny, because you just got your first standing ovation. If I waited for you to tell me when you were ready, I'd still be riding that stationary bike. It was time for you to step up and be on your own." Now, how profound was I?

Karl, who was now in sales at Xerox Corporation, and I had dinner one night. He was getting on me about the fact that there was no marketing and no promotions for the women's team. As a result, the crowds at Huff Hall, where we played, were down.

Just after the first of the year, I was doing a radio show, and the host thought it would be a great idea if I were to join the Polar Bear Club that year. As you may or may not know, the club caters to members who decide to take a jump into a lake in the middle of winter; that was not exactly high on my bucket list. However, the DJs were insistent that this was a great thing for this women's basketball coach to do.

If a marketing executive had approached me with the idea of promoting our basketball team by my taking a dip in the Lake of the Woods in January, I would have asked him to leave my office immediately. However, remembering the main reason for doing something was a cause, I thought about it for a moment and then said, "Okay. I'll jump into the lake with your Polar Bear Club if our next two games are sold out." We were playing Michigan State on Friday night and Ohio State on Sunday afternoon at home. If the DJs promoted our two games, and we sold out The Huff, I'd jump into the lake the following Tuesday morning. The DJs decided it would be just one game, but I had a cause. I wanted both games.

The DJs went to work and got their coworkers to promote this jump in the lake stunt on their shows. Everyone within earshot of that radio station knew that the crazy blonde from the East Coast was going to jump in the lake in the middle of January if the gym sold out that weekend.

I learned several things from that experience. First, the athletic director, Ron Guenther, called me and wanted to know if I was serious. I told him I was. I had given my word and couldn't back out now.

It was important to me that once I had said I was going to do something, to do it.

Then, the team doctor, Jeff Kyrauc, called and also asked if I was serious. I told him I was. He said I had to get to his office immediately because I needed a couple of shots before I jumped into the water. It was clear that the medical staff was not sure what was in the lake at that particular time of the year. But they knew I'd need a little extra protection.

Finally, I learned that when you say things in the locker room, or to a team privately, the players believe only so much. However, when you say it publicly, your team has a different take on things. Now, it was real. When my players found out that I really was going to jump in the lake if the two games were sold out, they decided to take on some responsibility. They didn't want to be at practice on Tuesday afternoon after we'd had a couple of losses from the weekend—and after I'd jumped in the lake.

Michigan State and Ohio State had their way with the University of Illinois women's basketball team for quite a while. For us to win both these games was going to take some doing and some playing on the part of my players.

Friday night came. We played Michigan State. The gym had a capacity of 4500 people. That night we had 4200 in the stands. The fire marshal was having an absolute fit. We beat Michigan State!

Sunday's game came. There were 4100 people in the gym. We beat Ohio State! The fire marshal was still not happy!

Tuesday came. It was fourteen degrees outside. Funny, when I'd met with the DJs a week before, it was forty-one degrees, and jumping in the lake didn't seem so bad. Now, it was a different story.

But Tuesday morning came, and I went to the Lake of the Woods. The radio station, TV stations, and the paramedics were all there. Oh, yes, the fire company trucks were there as well. No surprise: The lake was frozen. The fire company had to create a hole in the ice for me to jump into.

I've always been a God-fearing woman. I've always trusted in Divine Providence. Sometimes, I think I've trusted more than I was entitled to or should have. However, this day, the angels came, disguised as fraternity brothers. A carload of six arrived at the scene just as they were cracking the ice. They arrived with their Speedos and their ducky lifesaver rafts. As they proceeded to the lake, they proclaimed that they were there to help *me* jump. (I have to admit, I surmised that perhaps my wonderful fraternity brothers had imbibed a few libations before meeting me that morning. I never knew for sure, but it could have been the case.)

The six young men took flight. Into the lake they went—full body and under the water. I watched them. They were having an absolute blast. When they came out, the paramedics were there to cover them in blankets. Just to let you know how cold it was, their hair was frozen.

Oh my, what had I gotten myself into?

The radio station had been good sports about this because, technically, we did not have sellouts, so they were willing to let me off the hook. But we did have great crowds, and we did win two games, so I felt I had a responsibility to do something.

I took off my winter coat. I took off my sweat pants. I was left with only my shorts and a T-shirt. Thusly attired, into the lake I went.

There I was, standing in the middle of the lake, immortalized on the front page of the local newspaper.

The radio station kept its word and helped put a great crowd into Huff. My players kept their word and won two games that I don't believe too many people had penciled in as wins for us at the beginning of the season.

My angel friends from the fraternity assisted me with what probably was the dumbest thing I've ever done in my life.

And I kept my word and jumped into the water.

I cannot begin to tell you how cold that water was. But a deal is a deal.

I knew we had a team worth watching. I just needed to get the word out.

I just kept going, and the team followed me, all the way to the Big Ten championship. It was the most fun I ever had because I thought they'd begun to believe they could play. They weren't great athletes. They were real basketball players. We didn't have a lot of size, but we played power basketball. We raised the profile of the program.

And, we had fun doing it.

I've always loved dogs, but Karl didn't want one in the house. One day, I bought a ceramic dog, put him in the back of my car, and brought him home. He was big—one-hundred pounds—and expensive—he cost $300—and resembled a retriever. At first, Karl thought I had brought home a real dog. I called him Huff, after George Huff, the late Illinois athletic director. We played in Huff Hall. It wasn't much of a gym, but I thought it was the best place to play. I called it The Huff because all the great people and places in the world have "The" in front of their names: The Pope, The Vatican, The White House, The Palestra, The Ohio State University.

I brought Huff to practice every day for a week. I set him in the middle of the floor, and one of my managers kept an eye on him. The best part of Huff was that he never barked, never had to go for a walk, and didn't eat.

I still have him. He's in my living room today.

Shortly after Huff's arrival in my life, the Champaign SPCA called me about a possible—and real—rescue dog, a golden retriever named Buddy. Kevin and I adopted him, Karl came around, and Buddy became part of the Illinois program. I loved that dog because he was a lot like me. He was a golden retriever who didn't like the water, didn't retrieve, and pretended to have an injured paw so he could be carried places—by humans. He was an individual—stubborn, loyal—and he was *my* dog. If he didn't want to do something, he simply didn't do it. He went everywhere with me, even to practice.

My partner in crime was my youngest son, Kevin. I think he loved dogs more than I did. He would write his Christmas letters, and at the bottom, he would write, "But you know what I really want…"

My players used to say all the time, "Please, let us graduate before this dog dies."

• • •

For me, it wasn't all about the game, even though I was demanding about the National Championship all the time. In reality, as I look back, it's all about making a difference in people's lives. If you are a coach out there today, you have a responsibility to see the best in your players and develop their talent.

And a little attitude. During the 1997 season there was a picture of me in the paper, yelling at a referee. I looked a little demonic. The next day, Kathy McConnell took the picture, made copies of it, and posted it on every player's locker, and said to them, "Don't come out of the locker room unless you can match this intensity." I said to all my teams, "If you can match my intensity, we will be fine."

The picture made its way to a bagel shop in town with the caption, "Have you seen this woman?"

Intensity is essential. All my best teams had it.

I did all kinds of crazy things at Illinois. I continued the tradition of dressing up for practice on Halloween that I had started at Rutgers. One year, my staff and I were power rangers. We had helmets, hoods, gloves, and red, green, black, and yellow outfits. I chose black because it was the most slimming. We came in from all four corners of the floor. "Mighty Morphing Power Rangers." Here we were, in the middle of the gym. We were cracking up, and the players couldn't tell who was who until one player finally said, "I can tell Coach. I can tell by her diamonds." I love my diamonds.

Another time, we dressed up like characters in *The Wizard of Oz*. I was Glinda, the Good Witch of the North. That day, I coached in a tiara. And I led the parade when all the kids from campus came in.

I loved the band. When I'd arrived at Illinois, the band didn't play at women's games because they thought they were boring. So, I built up a relationship with them. Karl and I threw a masquerade ball for all three hundred members at Memorial Stadium. I was a constant visitor at their practices. One day, they asked me to be part of their halftime show at one of our home football games. "We want you to save the Big Ten from Godzilla," the band director said to me.

It was hilarious. Godzilla—actually a guy dressed in a Godzilla outfit—was out there, eating Ohio State, eating Michigan State, and Michigan, and chomping his way through Purdue. Then, I came out wearing my Illini orange shoes, sweater, and sunglasses. I wrestled him, got thrown to the ground, then got up, attacked him, and wrestled him to the ground. All this, in front of eighty thousand people.

At that time of my life—my forties—I enjoyed that. Now that I'm a little older, do I want to do that? No. At forty-seven, I was thrilled to do it. It was a great way to promote the program.

When I was in Illinois, I even had my own TV show. It was a coaches show. But I didn't want it to be just any show. So, I did it live from a restaurant. Before me, I heard that Jackie Gleason was the last guy who did live TV. We won the sweeps in February. We beat *Seinfeld*.

For part of the show, I talked about the players. Ironically, my very last show, which aired on CSTV, before resigning at Illinois, was all about family. I filmed the show on Saturday morning, and it would air Sunday mornings and Thursday afternoons. Well, the Thursday before filming, Kathleen, Chuck, their three boys Brian, Brendan, and Kevin, and my mother flew out to Illinois and surprised me. So, on Saturday, I took the three boys with me to filming, and they were guests on my show. I ended my show by saying, "It's not about wins, it's not about rebounds. It's about family. And that's the most important thing." How fitting to have my three nephews around me as the cameras shut off, and the lights dimmed on my final coaching show.

One day, we broadcast from my house. I made cheese steaks because the host asked me what I missed about Philly, and I said cheese steaks. The next week, I got three cheesecakes. I said, "No, no. I said Philly cheese steaks," so I had a cooking show in my kitchen. Another time, we did a radio show from my kitchen, and a guy came in and made blueberry pancakes. When the wife of the host of the morning drive show had triplets, I filled in for Stevie Jay and did his show for a week. It was great fun, except for the part where I had to get up at the crack of dawn.

I've always been interested in cooking. I decided to turn my hobby into a fundraising venture for our team. I hosted a dinner where a gourmet chef and

I cooked for three hundred people at $100 a plate. I had a chef's outfit with my name embroidered on the white jacket. I had a great chef's hat, too. I felt like I looked like a real chef. Later, I auctioned off my chef's hat for $2,000. The rest of my outfit was on the auction block when I told Karl he'd better make a sizeable donation before I lost the rest of my clothing.

Success was all very new to this team. But, to their credit, each of them played her part, even the deepest sub.

Amiee Smith had been a walk-on when she'd arrived at Illinois. But, after the previous coach left, she was given a full scholarship to flesh out the roster. At the end of my first year—Amiee had completed her junior year—she asked to see me. She realized she wasn't one of the better players on the team and knew we were recruiting players who could take us to the next level.

To help upgrade the program, she offered to rescind her scholarship and go back to being a walk-on if she could remain on the team.

I had no idea how this would work out. Amiee didn't play much her final year, but she did so much more for our team. After she graduated, I found out how valuable she had been in the locker room, how she put out so many smoldering fires before they became five-alarm blazes. Her insight and calm demeanor were priceless to the team.

Aimee was a true believer in what we were trying to accomplish. She was willing to make a huge personal sacrifice to help us get there. On senior night, Amiee had a chance to play and scored two points. Not many, but those two simple points meant the world to me.

The fans must have been impressed by the way we played. My first year, we averaged 632 fans at The Huff. During our championship season, we averaged over 4,100 in league play. We put a record sold-out crowd of 16,000 into Assembly Hall for our final home game against Purdue for the first and only time in the program's history.

We advanced to the first of two consecutive NCAA Sweet Sixteens. We lost to unbeaten—and eventual National Champion—Connecticut, 78-73, in Iowa City. I watched my vision turn into reality that night.

So did Ashley.

"I've seen UConn on TV. I've dreamed so long of playing against them," she said. "This is what it's all about. Playing against them—and knowing that we could beat them."

The player who walked out of that early practice wound up being selected Big Ten Player of the Year and was an All-American. Later, I found out she'd told her teammates that she was going to be my first All-American at Illinois after my introductory press conference.

Ashley had both drive and passion. And she beat Duke—the school that passed on her—twice in her career at Illinois.

I was talking with her recently, and she told me the message that resonated with her was "Find a way"—the same thing my mother said to me when I was growing up. After college, she took a job with Teach for America in a poor school district in California. She put that saying on her bulletin board every day.

She was the first Illinois women's basketball player to have her jersey number (#32) retired.

Today, she is playing receiver with the Chicago Force of the Women's Football Alliance, as well as working as an assistant coach at North Central College in Naperville, Illinois. Her youth sports company, Dream Out Loud Sports, LLC, has an after-school program that promotes preserving our ecological legacy.

I enjoyed the 1997 team. We were actually building something with one senior, four juniors, and a bunch of talented freshmen like Tauja Catchings, who eventually became an All Big Ten selection herself. Ann Henderson, the lone senior who played, made sure the players participated in our summer workout program.

I talked to Kelly Bond, a freshman on the 1997 team, recently and asked her, "Did you ever doubt?"

"No," she told me. "We would go back to the dorms and complain occasionally, but we were all on the same page. We always wanted to make sure we brought the effort. You were teaching us leadership that we would use later on. It was all about holding each other accountable and picking each other up."

When I first got there, I didn't know the players, and they didn't know me. But I bought into them from the beginning, and they bought into me after that.

Ten years later, we got together for a reunion. We were celebrating, and one of my former players pulled out the card with the mustard seed from her wallet. Then, three or four more opened their wallets and pulled out their mustard seeds. They had carried it with them all that time. It was something they'd kept all their lives because it had meaning for them.

I knew then that I'd made a difference in their lives. That was a good feeling.

One year, Illinois produced a calendar of twelve interesting people on campus, including yours truly. It consisted of twelve MRIs of our brains.

I was March—Passion—with my brain scan identified.

Just my luck. I finally get to be a calendar girl, and they wanted me only for my brain.

At least the Women's Basketball Hall of Fame recognized the whole me when I was inducted in the Class of 2001. I was thrilled, honored, and humbled.

The induction ceremony was on June 9, 2001 in Knoxville, Tennessee. It was also the day of my parents' fiftieth wedding anniversary.

Nothing lasts forever.

I left Illinois in 2007 after twelve years, for a perfect storm of reasons.

Our program had slipped from an NCAA team to a WNIT team. I was struggling to relate to my players. For the first time, I really sensed a generation gap.

I believe coaches have a shelf life and that mine had reached its "sell by" date. It was time for me to leave.

On Good Friday, I was sitting at my desk, thinking.

Sandi, my secretary, said, "What's on your mind?"

"I'll be back," I said as I walked out of the office.

"I don't like that look on your face."

"I'll be back."

I went to Ron Guenther, the athletic director, and resigned on the spot, even though I had one more year to go on my contract.

I'm an Aries. I'd made my decision then and there, and I never looked back.

He said to me, "Theresa, in the summertime, when you are playing golf, you're going to want to be coaching."

"No. I'm done," I insisted.

He asked me to think about it and sent me out recruiting. It was my best recruiting trip ever. I had a blast; I talked to everybody. Then, the president called and said, "Look, we know you can coach. But we also know there are about seven jobs that have your name on them in our department."

I thanked him, but I knew it was time to leave Illinois.

I started this book talking about passion. I'd always been an "I can do this" person. Even after the Olympics, it was still there, but dormant. I'd been nervous about Illinois, but my passion for the game had returned. But now it was different. That passion didn't come back, so I decided to do the right thing—and at the right time. I stepped down. I can't do a half-baked job. My father would kill me.

After thirty-three years, I'd gotten to the point where I realized I didn't want to do this anymore. I knew—and you have to know—when it's time to make a change, so you can continue to be your full self.

But I left the cupboard very well stocked. The school had a chance to win the Big Ten Championship that year but lost in the Big Ten Tournament Championship game against Purdue.

About that time, there was a finance job opening at St. John's Chapel in Illinois. They wanted to talk to me about the vacancy. I gave them a salary number, figuring they'd never come up with it. They did. But I'd already decided to back go home to Philadelphia, so I passed on the job.

It took us three days to stage the house for sale. It sold quickly. Afterward, I said to Karl, "You know, Bears (I call him Bears), we have a beautiful home." And he said to me, "Sweetheart, I want to tell you something: You didn't live in this one. You didn't live in the last one, either. I hope you'll live in the next one."

Why I Did It

"Always teach. And, if you must, use words." — St. Augustine.

You really can go home again. I proved it.

I returned to my roots in suburban Philadelphia and took a job as the assistant to the president of Immaculata.

At one point, I was invited to address the students at my old grade school, Our Lady of Fatima, before they voted for student council members.

I told them to choose the most qualified candidates and to make sure they elected a leader they could follow. I also told the kids that if they were student-athletes, to make sure they attended their classes, did their schoolwork, and were courteous to their nuns and teachers.

I got an unexpected surprise when I met two young girls—Tiffany and Kayla Kilday—who lived in my old row house on Stratford Road in Glenolden. I told them I came from a family of five kids. There were two parents and a grandmother living with us, and there was only one bathroom.

I asked them if there was still only one bathroom.

They told me there was now a powder room in the basement. When I told my mother, she was envious.

I told the kids I'd played basketball in the multi-purpose room where the school assembly was held. I pointed to the church across the street and said I got married there.

Good memories of good times.

It was so much more innocent back then.

I remained at Immaculata for four years. During that time, the school temporarily went Hollywood when filmmakers came to campus and acquired the rights to our story. The movie was called *The Mighty Macs* and was based on the true story of our first AIAW championship run when I was a sophomore in 1971. The movie starred Oscar-winning actress Ellen Burstyn, Carla Gugino, and David Boreanaz (of *Bones*) and was released in 2011, on the fortieth anniversary of our first championship win.

Cathy Rush referred to the film as part *Sister Act*, part, *Hoosiers*, and part *A League of Their Own*.

It was a chance to relive past glories and reunite with old friends. It was also a chance to make some new ones after filming started in 2006. It was a chance for me to be in the movies. I had a cameo appearance as a nun.

I don't like to live in the past. When I heard about the film, I didn't have much interest in meeting the actresses. But, when we got together, the actresses were excited about meeting us. When I met Katie Hayek, the actress who played my character, Trish Sharkey, we formed an immediate bond. We had worn these leather bands on our wrists at Immaculata. The actresses had those bands on. They were trying their best to portray us.

Katie Hayek was a Division I player for the University of Miami. In high school, she'd led Lancaster Catholic in central Pennsylvania to a district title. She auditioned for the role of Trish Sharkey when she was just twenty-three. The day she got the role, she was diagnosed with Hodgkin's Lymphoma, a form of cancer that spreads through the lymph cells. Her oncologist wanted her to start chemotherapy immediately. The director made a decision that Katie would keep the role, and they would film the basketball scenes early enough so that the filming would not affect Katie's chemo treatments.

I was still coaching at Illinois at the time of the photo shoot, but before I went back to Champaign, I told Katie, "If you really want to be like me, learn to use this." And I gave her my wooden rosary. (At this point, I was not aware of Katie's health issues.)

Katie is a beautiful brunette who wore a wig throughout the filming of the movie, knowing that she would probably lose her hair during her treatments. There was just something about that young woman that immediately drew you to the good in this world. She personified the goodness of life. When we went to ESPN to do publicity for the film, Katie had on a magenta-colored blouse while I wore a dress with the same colors. When we rang the New York Exchange bell, we both wore blue. All by chance without any coordination on our parts. Just a kindred spirit.

Katie's first chemo treatment was naturally a nerve-wracking experience. Her mom went with her to the hospital. As the medical staff prepared Katie for the treatment, one of the other patients just successfully completed treatment. Everyone was celebrating this latest success, with a cake. Katie and her mom weren't really interested in eating cake, and by the time it was passed to them, there really wasn't much left. Katie's mom, Joann, looked down at the remains and started to cry. The blue and white icing spelled out the word 'Shank.'

I had known nothing of Katie's treatments until after the film had been released. During one of our radio interviews was when I first heard the story of Katie, her first chemo treatment, and the cake. Earlier in this book, I said there are no coincidences. Everything happens for a reason. There is a reason why we met. Meeting Katie and her family was a special gift in my life. Thanks, Katie!

Katie continued her treatments. After several months, she was declared to be in remission.

In December 2012, she was told the cancer was back. Again, she faced a life decision. This time, there were new, different treatments. But some had stronger side effects and consequences.

When I learned of Katie's situation, I wrote her a note. It was about not settling for jump shots. As a player, Katie understood what I was talking about. This time, she decided to write a blog about her experiences. Unlike the first time, she wasn't going to do this alone. She was going to share the experience with those who loved her. She called me to ask if she could share my letter in her blog. I told her to go for it.

I wrote:

> "Keep fighting, Katie! Don't settle for jump shots; make sure you take the ball and life all the way to the rim! When you play the game that way, you will get fouled and you will get knocked down. But that's all part of the game. Take your time, get back on your two feet, breathe, and make the foul shots. Find a way to score! Find a way to live! Find a way to share! Find a way! That has always been my motto...find a way!
>
> Happy New Year, Buddy!
> Make the most of each day!
>
> The Mighty Macs find a way to do the impossible, to beat all the odds, and to live to celebrate the victory! Good luck, you're one of us forever.
>
> Peace and joy,
> Theresa"

As of her last appointment in the spring of 2013, Katie is cancer-free. We will say a prayer of Thanksgiving and thank God for the many graces that He shed upon her life. And we will say a second prayer that if she needs to go again and take the ball to the rim, she won't be settling for jump shots.

She's doing well now. She's an aspiring actress who's had roles on TV shows like *One Tree Hill* and *Law and Order*.

My letter to her pretty much sums up my philosophy about basketball—and life.

The ultimate measure of a person is not where he or she stands in moments of comfort or convenience. It's where he or she stands during challenges and controversy. Katie showed she was bigger than her cancer. She beat it, came back, and went on with her life.

To me, that's the triumph of the human spirit.

As coaches, we always talk about taking players beyond where they think they can go.

Sometimes, players can do that for coaches, too.

I didn't choose the coaching profession. I was called to it. I never wanted to coach. I never thought I was smart enough to coach. I didn't understand it well enough to teach it to others. I could play, and I knew what to do in a game. But I didn't know the nuances and the ins and outs. I was called to do it. And the way I was called was because of the tragedy at Sacred Heart Academy.

That led to two years at St. Joseph's, nineteen at Rutgers, and twelve more at Illinois, with twelve years of international coaching thrown in. I was always coming to a crossroads.

I was speaking to a women's group about leadership, and I said that careers have a shelf life to them. The only thing you can do for the rest of your life is to truly live the life you were meant to share.

In coaching, all you get to do is be the caretaker because your players belong to someone else. And it's up to you to make them the best versions of themselves.

Faith is very important to me. It has sustained me throughout my life and been behind everything I did. When I lost the Olympics, I didn't know if I could come back without my faith. Life is difficult. But, if you have the right tools—including faith—you will survive, and even be able to help others.

To do what we do—to coach, to lead, to take people beyond what they can do by themselves—you can't do it by yourself. You need guidance. You have to believe in something solid. In my case, it is Christianity, a religion that has survived for 2,000 years. It isn't perfect, but, to me, it has stood the test of time. I thought that was important. I went to Mass every morning during my career and many times took the homilies home to my players.

I didn't care what kind of religion my players practiced. I just wanted them to believe in something, to stand for something, just as they knew I did.

I mentioned the prayer, "O God of Players," earlier in this book. I said that prayer for every team from college to the Olympics. I said to my players, "Ladies, this is something that has been part of my routine. I would like to share it with you. If this is something you don't subscribe to, I will certainly understand. You are more than welcome to stand outside until we finish."

No one ever left.

One year, I took a Big Ten All Star team to Europe for an exhibition tour. They asked me to make up cards for them with that prayer on it.

For me, a relationship with a higher being is important. Because the Catholic religion was so guilt-ridden, I don't think I ever had a one-on-one relationship with Christ. But I found his mother, Mary, to be very loving. I could go through her to get to Him.

It reinforces what I like to say: "Men are the law. Women are the love. Men rule. Women reign."

I knew I'd always had the will to win. Everyone always says they would love to win. Winning beats losing. If you ask one hundred people if they would rather win or lose, one hundred people will say they want to win. But, when you tell those same one hundred people what they have to do to win, ninety-nine will walk away.

Only one will do what it takes.

That person is a winner.

The will to win is special. It's instinctive, and it's inside you. It's one of the things that make you tick, and it can bring you great happiness. Let's face it. People want to be happy, and they are always looking for happiness. Winning alone does not make you happy—I found that out for myself. But winning with integrity, winning with your teammates, being able to sacrifice and get to your goal with your team, that is what makes the whole process worthwhile.

When I first started playing basketball, I learned to play with boys. And they cut me no slack. Either I did it the way they did it, or I wasn't chosen for the next team. It was a very simple rule: either you can play, and play hard, or you will not be chosen by your peers to play. That was the rule of the playground. In order to stay on the court, you had to win. Losers gave up the court, and a new team came on.

I learned at a very young age that I hated losing. I was simply not going to lose. When I kept the purity of the game in front of me, winning was a very special moment.

When I played at Immaculata and coached at St. Joe's, Rutgers, and Illinois, I never thought about winning, necessarily, but I certainly never thought we would lose. I recently read a book called *Finding the Winning Edge* by Bill Walsh. The book was graciously gifted to me by Greg Schiano, the former Rutgers football head coach. I've always appreciated what Greg did for Rutgers. The book is all about discipline and having a plan two major traits that define both Greg and my teaching characteristics. (It also had a bunch of football play that I didn't understand.) Having a plan and discipline is a great way to get through life. You will always face different trials and tribulations; have your plan ready, along with your anchors, and go for it!

Growing up, I led a pretty sheltered life. My parents never told me what I couldn't do; they told me what I could do: never quit and find a way. These are the two lessons that I've taken with me throughout my entire life. If I were going to be outside playing with the boys—doing what I wanted to do—I was going to do it as well as I could.

I watched sports on television. Whenever teams won championships—I didn't care whether it was basketball, baseball, or football—I really wanted to watch the celebration in the locker rooms.

I realized that because I'd experienced that championship moment in my own locker room, I belonged to a fraternity (sorority?) and could join in any winners' locker room for the rest of my life. Sometimes, I'd get very emotional, watching the players pour champagne over one another, talking about how great it was to win this championship, and all the memories of my past came flooding back. On many occasions, tears flowed down my cheeks. Even though I never cried when I won my own championships, now I was crying watching these athletes win theirs. There is nothing like winning a championship.

Trust me—I know.

I've said winning a championship is like your education; no one can take it from you. (Unless the champions have violated some rule. Then, sure enough, the NCAA will strike your name from the record book.)

My husband said that, many times, we won games because I used my will over the players and pushed them, or pulled them, to win. When you don't know what it's like to win, it's very easy to quit too soon. Then, you missed the best part of all your hard work.

My motto was, "It's not okay to play hard and lose." What does that mean? It's real simple. If our games lasted forty minutes, and my team played hard for thirty-six minutes and lost the game, that was bad. I didn't want to hear any part of my players' excuses. Many times, young people hear that their opponents are better than they are; therefore, they feel they cannot win.

Forget that nonsense! It was their five against our five. We went out with the attitude that we could do this and get it done. That was how my players played the game. When a player was distracted, she forgot the reason that she played the game—for the fun of it. And the fun came from winning and working to be the best version of herself.

To practice all week, to run up and down the court, to spend all this time working to play a game everyone expected me to lose, makes absolutely no sense to me.

I've always said that I think losing is the dumbest thing you could do. Let the other guy lose.

Think about that for a minute. Why would you put all that hard work into it, just so you could go out with the idea that winning is not a possibility. My hope is—and what I am teaching now— that young people will think a little bit differently, become the best versions of themselves, and go out to win.

Over the years, I've purchased the book *The World's Greatest Salesman* by Og Mandino, as presents for my players, usually at Christmas. Even though they might not have time to read the entire book, I wanted them to read the tenth chapter. This chapter talks about one thing—and one thing only: WE WILL WIN!!! He repeated that over and over and over again. After a while, when the players began to see it in writing, and they read it aloud, they started to really believe it. WE WILL WIN!!!

Many of my players became coaches—some of them even took my place. When they coached their own teams, they didn't even bother to change the name of a play I had taught them. When I asked them why they kept the name, they said, "Why change the name? It worked before. It works for us."

That just shows you never really know the impact you have on other people.

When I was coaching and found myself in a tough spot with players who'd never been in that situation before, I'd tell them what was going to happen next. And, most of the time, it happened exactly as I'd said it would. I don't think I'm clairvoyant or have a crystal ball. But, I do think that, as a coach, I planted positive seeds in my players' minds, and they made it happen. We're going to steal the inbounds pass and score, then go right back into a full court press and change the momentum of the game by stealing the ball again.

The best part of doing this was looking into the eyes of my players. They believed every word of it.

The will to win is also about confidence. Life is a self-fulfilling prophecy. If you think you can, you will. If you think you can't, you won't.

And this is why I decided to go back to my first love—teaching basketball to young kids.

As a coach, I had to deal with grades, moods, players who didn't want to play, off-the-court problems, school administrators, pressure to win, and graduation rates. Teaching is freedom from all that. Teaching is the instruction of individuals by care and empathy. In teaching, you employ the quiet listening skills of both the ears and the heart. I find kids are with me because they want to be there.

Teaching is just like everything else that happened in my life. I didn't plan on this. It was divine providence. My real plan was to retire and maybe play golf, and perhaps even volunteer at the local SPCA. But somehow I ended up creating Grentz Elite Coaching, a teaching academy of the fundamentals of the game of basketball.

Everybody is gifted. Everyone has all kinds of gifts. Unfortunately, people don't always see those gifts. They don't realize how gifted and talented they are. They're looking at what other people have instead of taking a really in-depth look at themselves. I have a lot of unique and good things I can offer to others. In my case, I know I liked going to practice and talking to kids.

Once again, my life was called to a direction I did not plan. I became a third volunteer assistant coach at Villa Maria, a private Catholic girls' academy near Malvern, Pennsylvania.

I sat on the bench—where the players were. When they'd come out of the game, I'd tell them that this is what the coach said. This is what she meant. And this is what you are going to do. Then, I told them to go in the game and do their best. That became our thing. What I really liked about it was there was no age difference in their view. They just saw me as "Coach T."

I wasn't trying to persuade them to do anything. I just told them what they needed to do. We weren't trying to create any great friendship. They had no idea who I was. And it was much better that way.

Once the movie about "The Mighty Macs" came out, though, they started to figure out who I was.

After the season, a few parents came and said to me, "Coach, we all voted. We think it would be great if you coached the girls in the summer, in the AAU league."

I told them no.

They said, "No, no, no. We'll do all the work. You coach them."

I was insistent it wasn't going to happen. I said, "I'm not going to coach them, but I will teach them."

And that's what I've been doing at Grentz Elite Coaching.

Nobody wants to teach basketball the way I do because you won't make a lot of money doing this, and you must put a lot of time into doing it. Coaches would rather put eighty kids on the floor during several hours of lessons as opposed to take two hours and put two kids on the floor—and do it four times a day.

I enjoy teaching. I'm sixty-one now. But, when I'm on the floor, nothing hurts. When I come off the floor, I can just about move. I want to stay as close to the floor as I can. And this job helps me do that. What I like about this is how enthusiastic and eager the kids are. They want to learn. What I'm teaching them is not the basic drills over and over again.

I don't teach plays. I teach how to play.

I tell them, "Keep an open mind and enjoy learning." Practice means to LEARN.

L stands for listen. Listen and pick up on what is being said. And remember it.

E stands for experiment. Take a chance and try new things, but at the proper time.

A stands for awareness. Be aware of your surroundings and your teammates. React accordingly.

R stands for repetition. If you want to master a movement or a motion, you have to do it ten thousand times.

N stands nuggets of wisdom. Coaches have them. Pay attention to them.

Teaching is a lost art. It's all about how many games can we play and recruiting.

With so many parents, it's all about the scholarships.

With me, I invite the parents in to watch our sessions because what I teach is often overlooked in regular practices. High School coaches and AAU coaches don't always have time to teach the individual skills to players in the programs. Court time is like gold. There are so many teams out there today and so many leagues that need gym time. Unfortunately, the individual skills of the players are pushed to the side. I teach concepts like thinking about the percentage of your shot, the idea of catching the ball and immediately looking at the basket. What is the first thing kids do when they catch the ball? They look down or dribble. The type of basketball player a kid becomes is based on her habits.

But people don't have habits; they have instincts. I teach the kids to have the best habits possible.

When you get in a tough situation on the court, you will revert to your habits. In our sessions, I try to instill the proper mechanics and fundamentals of ball handling and dribbling. Knowing how to do dribbling drills does not mean you know how to drive the basketball to the rim. These are all processes that take an inordinate amount of time to learn and to practice.

When you catch a ball, the first thing you do is dribble it or shoot it. What I've learned over the past several months are some new things—like the positioning of the arm—which I never worried about before. In looking at pictures on the Internet, I discovered that the great players always have their arms at a certain angle. It's very natural to drop your arm—that is where it's supposed to be. When you start lifting your forearm and keeping your elbows away from your body, it works. But you have to start living outside your comfort zone. You have to learn to become comfortable outside of your comfort zone.

People will come only so far. Why? Because people are inherently lazy. These are all things I'm learning that I try to impart to my students. The earlier I get them, the easier it is to change those habits.

It's all about creating positive habits that will allow you to become a great player.

I think a lot of the traits I teach—passion, intensity, loyalty, leadership, accountability, desire, courage, self-discipline, humility, respect, trustworthiness, work ethic, and determination—are traits I look for in myself first, and then try to find in others. When I went recruiting, I wanted young women who personified my twelve characteristics for success. I call them my string of pearls. They are all linked, and together, like a necklace, each one enhances and beautifies the others in the chain.

I discovered an important fact during the time I've been teaching—kids need discipline. They need to learn self-discipline and self-sacrifice. It doesn't matter what era the kids are from—kids need discipline. I think that is especially true today when they aren't getting it at home. The players I first coached didn't have a credit card and didn't have a car—or it was a clunker. Today's kids have a credit card, have a new car, have a cell phone; they have everything. And, for the most part, it's been handed to them.

At the end of my coaching career, if we lost a game, it was no big deal. They were still taking a charter flight home and weren't missing any meals. They asked me, "What are you so upset about?"

This is when I realized the generation gap had begun between my players and me.

And it continues today.

Everything now is about scholarships, scholarships, scholarships.

Let me share a story with you. I was recruiting a player from Chicago who was playing on a top soccer team that was playing a tournament in Disneyland. Because I was a basketball coach, none of the parents knew me, so I was able to go to the game and observe. I actually "ear hustled" on a couple of their conversations. Bad Theresa!

Talking about their daughters, one mother said she had counted the schools that were there. Another said it was all about getting her child's name on the National Letter of Intent.

That was eye opening to me. This is what parents want. But what about the kids? What do they want?

I know college is expensive, but too many kids today play for the money, not for the joy of the game.

Young kids don't think that way, but because of the pressure on them, they think, Okay, if I'm scoring points, someone will recruit me. Some parents have played in college on scholarships, and they've told their daughters things they think need to be done to secure a free ride. There is no such thing as a "free ride."

What made my great teams great was that when we failed, we got back up. Nobody interfered. We made mistakes. But they were ours to make and learn from. The more the parents stayed away, the better the kids grew. As I moved further along in my career, more parents got involved. Now, their kids weren't allowed to fail. Name me one person who has become an automatic success.

Today's parents are teaching failure: my kid can't fail; my kid's not wrong. You have to fail; it's the only way you learn.

Trust me. I know.

Since I've starting teaching, I've observed girls' lack of self-confidence. When does it start? Why do they give up their interest in math and science? Why do so many parents allocate it to others to instill self-confidence in their daughters? I'm no sociologist, but as a teacher, I feel my job is to get these kids to feel good about themselves and their abilities. To play is to win. I refer back to Mary Sue Garrity Simon's remarks about confidence.

I feel both blessed and obligated to be in a position to give back. Let's face it. We are the past. The future is staring us in the face. And it's coming from players who want to learn how to play. We owe it to them to smooth their paths.

Forty-five years ago, I was starting out, and each step was a new adventure; learning to compete against the boys was not the norm. Now, girls can do that. Sports are more accepting of women. There are scholarships and jobs after college. I motivate my students to be the best they can be because I still believe life is a learning experience.

I embarked on a life-long journey of self-discipline—both as a person and as a coach. I'm still traveling.

If I've helped these young women learn the principles that have worked for me, then my life has been a success.

Author Biography

Theresa Shank Grentz is a member of the Women's Basketball Hall of Fame, who served as the US Olympic head coach in 1992. Over the course of thirty-three years, she worked as the head women's basketball coach for the University of Illinois, Rutgers University, and St. Joseph's University.

She got her start playing for the Immaculata Mighty Macs, and led the team to three AIAW National Championships between 1972 and 1974. These events were made into a movie, *The Mighty Macs*, which was released in 2011.

Throughout her coaching career, she has shown a knack for motivational speaking, and has given over one thousand speeches to various groups—from kindergarten classes, to Fortune 500 companies.

Grentz is the owner of Grentz Elite Coaching, a basketball-teaching academy located in West Chester, Pennsylvania. Through the academy, she has run clinics and camps all over the United States.

Made in the USA
Lexington, KY
03 June 2014